The complete traveller's guide

Distributed by:

UK
A.A. Publishing
(A Division of the
Automobile Association)
Fanum House
Basingstroke
Hampshire RG21 2EA

Australia
Gordon & Gotch Ltd,
25-37 Huntingdale Road,
Burwood
Victoria 3125

Tourist Publications

First published and produced
in Australia in 1990 by:

T.P. Books & Print Pty Ltd
Suite 13, 3 Moore Lane
Harbord Village
Harbord NSW 2096

In Association with:

Tourist Publications
6 Pilliou Street
Koliatsou Square
112 55 Athens, Greece

Editorial Directors:	L. Starr
	Y. Skordilis
Author:	Kerry & Geoff Kenihan
Typography:	M. Roetman
Design:	C. Mills
Layout:	C. Mills
Photosetting:	Deblaere Typesetting Pty Ltd
Photographs:	Canadian Consulate General Sydney
Maps:	Judy Trim

Printed in Australia

ISBN 1 872163 50 5

Due to the wealth of information available, it has been necessary to be selective. Sufficient detail is given to allow the visitor to make choices depending on personal taste, and the information has been carefully checked. However, errors creep in and changes will occur. We hope you will forgive the errors and omissions and find this book a helpful companion.

ABOUT THIS GUIDE

Toronto, the city that works, has also been called the People City. Vital, cultured, cosmopolitan, sporting in all senses of the word, safe and populated by more than 70 different national groups, Canada's largest metropolis is a place to enjoy in the fast lane or relax by the shores of Lake Ontario.

Part I tells how Canada came to be, how its history was etched out by courage, and explains its spectacular geography, geology, flora, fauna, method of government, etc.

Part II takes you on an exploration of Toronto's two cities, above ground and along the largest subterranean complex in the world. It also directs you to the world's honeymoon capital, fabulous Niagara Falls which, on a clear day, can be seen from the earth's highest free standing structure in Toronto, the CN Tower.

Part III recommends the best places to stay, no matter what your budget.

Part IV illustrates how to make the city that works work for you, practical information on how, why, when and what and where to gain assistance if necessary.

Part V, while aimed to make the business traveller's visit a breeze, will also help holiday-makers with additional practicalities.

Toronto. You'd never believe it was once conventionally reserved. There is something to experience at every turn, no matter your interests or pre-disposition. You won't be disappointed.

ACKNOWLEDGEMENTS

The authors are most grateful to the **Canadian Consulate General**, particularly 'Mr Andrew Hunter' in Sydney, and **Mr Barry Eaton** of **Eaton Enterprises**, Sydney for their encouragement and informative support in the preparation of this InfoGuide. We also wish to thank **Canadian Airlines International** for transport to, from and within Canada and **Ansett Airlines** for internal connecting flights in Australia.

Table of Contents

PART I - CANADA AND ITS PEOPLE

A Spirit of Pioneering 9
Geology and Geography 12
Climate 13
Flora and Fauna 13
Government 16
Education 16
Commerce and Industry 17
Religion 19
The Canadian People 19
Meeting People 21
Language 21
From Settlement to the Space Age 24
Toronto, More than a Capital 30

PART II - TORONTO - NIAGARA FALLS

A Cinderella City 37
Toronto Islands 40
At the Heart of it All 40
Harbourfront 42
Maritime Museum 43
Canadian National Exhibition 44
Hockey Hall of Fame and Museum 44
Ontario Place 45
Scadding Cabin 45
Fort York 46
Baseball Hall of Fame and Museum 46
Colborne Lodge 47
High Park 47
Beaches Park 48
Redpath Sugar Museum 48
Scarborough Bluff 48
Toronto Zoo 49
CN Tower 50
Skydome 51
Toronto Stock Exchange 53
City Hall 54
Campbell House 54
Art Gallery of Ontario 54
The Grange 55
Chinatown 56
Parliment Building 56

China Court 56
Sigmund Samuel Building 57
University of Toronto 58
McLaughlin Planetarium 58
Royal Ontario Museum 58
George R Gardiner Museum 60
Casa Loma 61
Museum of the History of Medicine 61
Metropolitan Toronto Library 62
Spadina House 62
Yorkville 62
Metropolitan Toronto Police Museum 64
Allan Gardens 64
Mackenzie House 65
Eaton Centre 65
Toronto's First Post Office 68
Massey Hall 68
St Lawrence Centre 68
O'Keefe Centre 69
Market Gallery 69
BENEATH THE STREETS 70
BEYOND DOWNTOWN 72
SIDE TRIPPING 79
NIAGARA FALLS 81
OFF TO OTTAWA 92

PART III - ACCOMMODATION
Hotels & Camping Sites 99

PART IV - PRACTICAL INFORMATION
A-Z Summary 114

PART V - BUSINESS GUIDE
.... 183

MAPS
Toronto 94-95
Canada 190-191

INDEX 192

PART I
General Introduction

Old City Hall

CANADA AND HER PEOPLE

A SPIRIT OF PIONEERING

Canada's symbol is the maple leaf. On its transition through the spectrum of the changing seasons, it represents the variety of vibrant hues to be found in this land of immense scenic grandeur green, yellow, gold, red, russet and brown. As a bare, almost black twig in winter, the leaf is etched against a sky of blue and a backdrop of purest, white snow. All these are the colours of Canada.

The spectrum too reflects the colours of skin of Canada's diverse peoples, some natives of the country which is second in size only to the U.S.S.R.; most descendents of pioneers from Europe who began arriving on Canadian shores in the 15th century. They followed the wake of **Leif Ericsson's** Viking longship which had made a Canadian landfall nearly 500 years before.

With the exception of Alaska, which belongs to the United States, Canada and its lovely off-shore islands occupies the top of the North American continent. Larger than the U.S.A. by 200,000 square miles, it sweeps across 3.8 million square miles. Yet while this nation is so large, it is home only to 26 million people, most of whom are concentrated in the southern major cities which are not only beautiful, well-planned and sophisticated, but are extremely safe for travellers and residents alike.

All of these cities offer interesting, cosmopolitan, cultural and sporting experiences and activities to rival those of the United States and Europe.

In addition, Canada has an awe-inspiring variety of scenery from the fjord-like waterways beneath snow-capped mountains on the east coast. The dauntingly majestic Rockies, the colourful patchwork of the prairies, forests of pine, and the tranquility of the Great Lakes to the splendour of the irrepressible Niagara Falls. There are also the Northwest Territories and the mysterious Yukon where hundreds of remote lakes, unnamed and not mapped, extend like sapphire jewels cast down across a rugged wilderness towards the Arctic Sea which few people have explored. Canada is divided into 12 provinces and territories -British Columbia, gateway to visitors arriving from across the Pacific, the Yukon, Northwest Territories, Alberta, Saskatchewan, Manitoba, Ontario, Quebec, New Brunswick, Nova Scotia, Prince Edward Island and Newfoundland.

Newfoundland is the youngest of Canada's provinces. While the Irish and the Poles may be the butt of harmless humour in other parts of the world, Canada's equivalent are the **Newfies** of Newfoundland, renowned for their pioneering spirit and their warmth of hospitality.

But hospitality is not just confined to this province. The concept is endemic in the nation.

Canada's major cities are, from west to east, vital **Vancouver** where one in every four families owns a boat to cruise about 5000 miles of sheltered waterways, and Alberta's Edmonton which boasts the world's largest shopping mall almost a city within a city. **Ontario's** Toronto, the great city you will explore through this guide book, is a dynamic metropolis set on the shores of Lake Ontario and a short distance from the world's honeymoon capital, **Niagara Falls**.

Toronto shares the same province with the nation's capital, **Ottawa** where the guards which change at the Parliament Building appear to have been plucked straight out of Buckingham Palace. Ottawa, with its lovely **Rideau Canal** along which skaters commute to town in winter, has close ties with The Netherlands.

Dutch Queen Beatrix, sheltering there during the Second World War, was about to have the infant Princess Marguerite. As a gesture of friendship, the city fathers made Ottowa Dutch territory for a day so that the baby could retain her nationality. Since then, Queen Beatrix has sent an annual gift of thousands of tulips to add to the magnificent blooms which are displayed each year in Canada's tulip capital.

The two other great cities of Canada are **Montreal** and **Quebec**, both very French and sophisticated and in the pretty province of Quebec. It was in Quebec city, on the banks of the St. Lawrence River that French Canada was founded by **Samuel de Champlain**.

In the eastern provinces, you will find the greatest French influences - language, customs, architecture and cuisine. But in deference to the somewhat stand-offish reputation that the French in France have established for themselves among some foreign visitors, you will find that if you do not speak or read French in Canada, French-speaking Canadians will be friendly and helpful to you - and will speak English also.

Particularly in Quebec, road signs, menus and tourist information are in both languages.

Above all, Canada is a nation of unique contrasts, scenically and culturally. Despite its relatively small population, it has such tourist attractions as world-class theme parks, game reserves, booming theatre towns, year-round festivals and the largest subterranean shopping complexes on Earth.

Its accommodations, restaurants, transport systems, both urban and long-distance, are equal and often superior to those of the United States, and the most advanced nations of Europe. With a dare-devil and courageous pioneering history of aviation, its distances are closed by efficient air services.

There is also a surprise. Unlike most public facilities in the Western world, the visitor will not find any in Canada defaced by graffitti or vandalized. It is a nation with one of the world's lowest crime rates.

Green and burgeoning in spring, vital and bustling in summer, presenting an amazing autumn which has to be seen for its almost unbelievable beauty, and a winter sports playground, which can be enjoyed in cosmopolitan company or the splendid isolation of the wild, Canada is truly a land for all people through all seasons.

Sand Dunes Bay

GEOLOGY AND GEOGRAPHY

Canada is the largest nation by area in the western hemisphere and the second largest in the world. Geologically, it can be compared with a huge, roughly rectangular dish, the centre of which is the shallow **Hudson Bay** hedged in to the north, west and east by mountains.

The country's eastern mountain chain culminates in Newfoundland and, in the south, joins with the Appalachian Mountains of the United States. This relatively low chain follows the border between the state of Maine and the province of Quebec, continuing through the Gaspe Peninsula and across western Newfoundland.

Canada's eastern coastal plain is extremely narrow. But, geologically, it extends into the Atlantic, creating a very wide, Continental shelf off Nova Scotia and Newfoundland. The northern-most arm of Canada's Eastern Mountains forms the coast of Labrador and continues northward to the east coast of Baffin Island where some peaks exceed 8,000 feet in height.

The western area of Canada is part of the great Rocky Mountains system which extends from Panama in the south to Alaska in a general north-west-south-east line.

The ranges are not as wide in Canada as they are in the United States but the valleys are narrower and deeper than those encountered south of the border. Tending north-westwards, the great Rockies of Canada continue through the Yukon and finally split into several distinctive ranges in Alaska.

Contained by these two great mountain systems is the vast interior basin of lowlands. Glaciation during the great Ice Ages has resulted in a huge number of lakes, the largest of which occur around Hudson Bay although the most famous are those of the St Lawrence river system, generally referred to as the **Great Lakes**. In terms of geography, Canada, with the exception of Alaska, comprises all of the continent north of the 49th parallel of latitude between the Pacific Ocean and the Lake of the Woods. The frontier of the Unites States then follows a chain of small lakes to the mouth of the Pigeon River on the north west of Lake Superior and, from there, roughly eastward to the American state of Maine where the latitude is about 45 degrees.

CLIMATE

Because of its enormous size, and particularly the north-south degrees of latitude that Canada occupies, there are huge climatic variations. In general terms, spring begins in the middle of March, summer in mid-May, autumn half-way through September and winter from the middle of November.

Mean summer temperatures can vary from 67 degrees Fahrenheit in the Northwest Territories to 81 degrees in Ontario. The average winter temperatures range from -26 degrees in the north-west to a relatively mild 31 degrees in British Columbia.

There can be considerable climatic variations within the 12 provinces and territories. Ontario, in which Toronto lies, has a temperature range averaging -2 degrees in winter to 81 degrees in summer, (Fahrenheit)

FLORA AND FAUNA

While Canada's great climatic variations resulted in a diversity of flora, generally, with the exception of the prairie grasslands and the Arctic tundras, the country, before European settlement, could be compared with a vast and mainly coniferous forest.

Commercial logging and clearing for agriculture has denuded much of the nation's stands of red cedar but from British Columbia in the west to Nova Scotia in the east, some of the finest pine forests of the world can still be found. Particularly in the national parks, with which Canada abounds, can be seen a range of forest trees including red spruce, balsam, white and red pine, hemlock, maple, birch, ash. elm, spruce, poplar, aspen, oak, cedar, and fir.

Wildflowers are everywhere and it is a wonderful sight to• see them springing up from the roadside against a setting of a clear, blue lake and a craggy mountain crisped with snow in spring, summer or autumn.

The national parks are also pure paradise for visitors who are fascinated by safe encounters with Canada's wild animals. Depending on the location, these include caribou, moose, deer, antelope, elk, black, grizzly and polar bears, wolf, cyote, cougar, the common and the silver fox, lynx, mouflon, wild goat, marmot, beaver, otter, marten, mink, squirrel - and a score or more other small, furred creatures.

There are also seals and walruses in the remote seaside tundra regions.

INFOTIP: If you are camping in a tent or picnicking after a hike in a national park, do store your food in the odd-looking food caches which are suspended high between two poles. These are plentiful in park camp areas. Grizzly and black bears can wander freely though the parks. With your supplies safely out of reach, the bears will not become habitues to human food and, therefore, possibly aggressive. Also, take your rubbish with you or deposit it in sealed bins for the same reason.

Some highways, particularly in the province of Alberta between December to June 15, are closed in respect of the habits of the elk and deer which need to move freely from winter to summer, without the threat of traffic, down to lower ground to find food and calve. There will be alternative routes.

INFOTIP: When hiking in the mountains and/or national parks, wear bells around your ankles, especially in spring. Grizzly and black bears tend to climb trees to escape humans but, in spring, they are very protective of their new-born young and their territories so it's wise to let them know you are coming.

Canada's prolific birdlife is mostly migratory. Most species are common to the northern areas of the United States from the Atlantic to the Pacific. Eagles, hawks and owls are still numerous in the mountains and forested areas. Song birds are found everywhere in the forests. Canadian seabirds are mostly the same as those found around the coastlines of northern Europe and Great Britain.

You'll see penguins along the shores of the Yukon and Northwest Territories and also northern Quebec.

And the fish abound in the Atlantic and Pacific seas - tuna, bass and the famed salmon - and team through streams, rivers and lakes in every imaginable freshwater variety. Fishing is one of Canada's prime sporting activities, one of the finest being the fly-in experience of being dropped by aircraft to a remote area for the catch of a lifetime.

Eaton Centre

GOVERNMENT

Canada is an independent nation of the British Commonwealth of Nations and, formal executive power rests with a Governor General who represents the Queen of England. The Governor General has the power to summon and dissolve Parliament and gives the royal assent to all legislation by the Federal Parliament which is in the city of Ottawa.

That is the limit of his power. In practice, the Governor General acts only on the advice of the Prime Minister and his cabinet ministers who are all elected members of Canada's two houses of parliament - the Commons and the Senate. The Prime Minister is invariably the parliamentary leader of a political party which has a majority of members in the Parliament.

Canada's provincial governments or State Governments are financed mainly through a share of federal revenue supplemented by local taxes, for example, revenue from petrol sales, liquor and death duties.

There is a third or local tier of government covering the day to day affairs of towns and cities. The system is similar to that of the United Kingdom and the other countries of the British Commonwealth whose democratic system of government stems from the Westminster system of England and the traditions of England's county councils.

EDUCATION

In Canada, public education is free and co-educational up to and including secondary school. Children are required by law to attend school from the age of six or seven until they are 15 or 16 years old.

The administration of the education system is provincial and each province has developed its own elementary and secondary school system. In Quebec, free education is extended to include the general and vocational colleges but most other post-secondary education has to be paid for.

A Canadian child's schooling often starts in kindergarten and usually lasts at least 10 years. University entrance requirements vary from province to province. Canada has more than 60 universities attended by nearly 400,000 full-time and 250,000 part-time students. There are another 200 post-secondary institutions attended by more than 250,000 students. Nearly 35,000 foreign students go to Canadian universities. Toronto's university is Canada's largest.

COMMERCE AND INDUSTRY

If a single word can describe the Canadian economy, it is diversified.

Canada is a technologically-advanced nation with sophisticated industrial and manufacturing sectors. But it is also a major exporter of raw and semi-processed materials. Canadian exports range from short-takeoff-and-landing (STOL) aircraft and diesel trains to oil and wheat - a diversification that has provided Canada with a number of opportunities and choices not normally available to other advanced world economies.

Canada's earliest economic activity involved the fur trade, fishing, forestry and farming. The opening-up of Western Canada was very largely the result of the pursuit of the declining beaver population. Fishing off the Grand Banks and off Canada's extensive east coast as well as in its lakes and rivers became another major source of food and provided a livelihood for a large proportion of the population.

National Exhibition

In the days of sail, the ships of the British Royal Navy spread their canvas on masts of Canadian timber.

By the beginning of the 20th century, Canada's prairies had become a granary for the world.

As Canada prospered, it depended less and less on primary industry. Manufacturing and industrial firms grew rapidly - an expansion stimulated by a large injection of foreign capital, particularly from the United States. At first, most secondary industry was centred in the St Lawrence Valley and the Great Lakes region. But since the first decade of this century, it has spread across the nation from the Atlantic to the Pacific.

Manufacturing is the largest of Canada's secondary industries and it is highly mechanized. The nation's factories constitute a large market for investment capital and capital equipment. This trend has been reinforced by the fact that most Canadian industries either produce highly-manufactured goods such as motor vehicles, machinery and aircraft, or are involved in the processing of natural resources - both of which operations are capital-intensive.

The extent and technical expertise of Canadian industry can best be appreciated by naming nine major areas; aviation, automobiles, heavy machinery, electrical and electronic goods, iron and steel, urban transport systems, farming, fishing and forestry and mining.

RELIGION

Canada is overwhelmingly a Christian nation with about half of the total population Catholic. There is also a strong Protestant following with the Uniting and Anglican churches having the largest numbers of adherents.

The eastern Orthodox forms of Christianity represent the beliefs of Ukrainians and Greeks and their descendents in particular. Well over 250,000 people adhere to the Jewish faith. An even greater number subscribe to other Eastern non-Christian religions.

THE CANADIAN PEOPLE

The Americans justify their multi-culturalism as a melting pot but the Canadians have a different view. They promote the ethnicity of individual national groups which have migrated to their country.

Because of this attitude, you will find areas which are as English as England. How about the Shakespeare Festival at Stratford, Ontario or the Shaw (as in George Bernard) Festival at Niagara-on-the-Lake where the bed and breakfast accommodations could have come out of England's Cotswolds? You'll find Ukrainians and their traditions in Alberta's Edmonton and across Manitoba; little Italys and Chinatowns in several cities.

But, opposing the concept of concentrations, (there are certainly no ghettos in Canada) different ethnic peoples also live harmoniously together. For example, in just one street in Toronto, there are restaurants which represent about 70 different national cuisines and most owners live in the same area.

The **French** and the **English** followed the **Vikings** to join, not always happily, the native nomadic **Indians** and the **Eskimos** (Inuit).

Canada's first European explorers came immediately in contact with the native people of the North American continent. Because of their dark brown skin, they called them Indians. This name could not be applied to the people who were later discovered dwelling in the Arctic regions of Canada and the term Eskimo was used to describe them.

The Canadian Indians do not differ in any essential way to the tribes of the United States and they are characterized by smooth, lank hair, broad faces and prominent cheek bones. While the hair of the Eskimo people is similar in texture and colour, their skin is a lighter brown, their heads are longer and narrower and their faces, generally, appear flatter than those of the Indians to the south.

The mythology of both the Indians and Eskimos is rich, filled with stories of superhuman deeds and deities. Anthropologists estimate that more than 200,000 Indians inhabited Canada at the time of European discovery and settlement. This number greatly declined under the impact of European diseases to which the Indians lacked natural immunity. But unlike their related tribesfolk in the United States, Canada's Indians did not suffer the wars and massacres which occurred in America.

Today, the Indian population exceeds 285,000 and Canadian Indians are prominent in virtually every area of the nation's life. Many of them live in the nearly 600 separate Indian communities scattered across Canada sharing more than 2000 reservations. A very few still lead a nomadic lifestyle in the far northwest.

More and more, the Canadian Indians are re-discovering and preserving their cultural heritage. The Indian languages are taught in many of the schools that are administered by the native communities.

Ethnic Groups

MEETING PEOPLE

One has only to pause on a street anywhere and look quizzically at a map and a Canadian will be instantly at your side asking if he or she can assist you. The Canadian people are so friendly and welcoming of visitors that it is impossible not to meet them, be it on the street, across tables at a restaurant, at a hotel check-in desk, a sporting meeting, on public transport, or because you have attended a musical or cultural performance in which they, too, are interested.

Camping, hiking, in fact anywhere in Canada's great and spectacular outdoors, you will find people proud of their nation and therefore willing to impart information and friendship which will make your stay more pleasurable.

Because Canada - and we emphasize - is such a safe country, you will not find the reserve towards strangers that has, disappointingly emerged in other nations because of their increasing street crime rates. Stop at any one of the hundreds of Toronto's sausage stalls (the sausages are all made to different, individual recipes,) and you will be in instant conversation with a Canadian who, likely as not, will also tell you about his European or Middle Eastern heritage. Example: One of this guide's authors stopped for a sausage snack in front of a Toronto Museum and was confused by the variety of accompaniments which could go at no extra charge with her sausage in a bun. 'Are you English, or Australian? New Zealander?' the vendor queried. This led to an exchange about respective countries and the offer to try absolutely ALL of the pickles, sauces and assorted garnishes that could turn a simple sausage into a memorable lunch on the run - which it was!

You will never feel lonely in Canada even if you are travelling solo.

LANGUAGE

Almost 50 per cent of Canadians have British heritage while about 30 per cent claim ancestry from France. The remaining 20 per cent are from everywhere else. But in Ontario and Toronto in particular, you will not need to carry a French phrase book, nor will you in the more Gallic provinces, such as Quebec, where almost everyone speaks English as well as French. But if you have a second language - from Chinese Mandarin to Greek - in your repertoire, you will find opportunity to practise it in Toronto, particularly in the varied restaurants.

Festival of Spring, Ottawa

FROM SETTLEMENT TO THE SPACE AGE

No one knows exactly how long Canada has been populated but it is a certainty that the indigenous people, the **Inuit**, or Eskimos, have been a hardy race to survive millennia of harsh, high Arctic, snow-bound winters. These are the people about whom older readers learned at school, lived in **igloos**, cracked whips over huskies drawing their sleds and paddled their **kayaks** through ice floes in search of fish, seal, walrus and polar bear.

About 30,000 years ago, Canada was ice-covered and Alaska was linked with Siberia. Archaeologists believe that today's Inuit are descendent from the **Thule Eskimo** people of **Greenland**.

Because the Inuit were isolated from the rest of the world, they believed they were alone on earth. The word Inuit means people. Then, Viking, French and English explorers made sporadic contact with these people, but until the 19th century their way of life had changed little over thousands of years. It is believed that the Inuit, who lived along the Arctic Ocean, the southern **Great Lakes** and around what is now Vancouver Island and also Labrador and Newfoundland in the east, first met Iceland's Norsemen when they arrived on Canada's east coast about 1000 years ago.

Some 600 years later, English and French adventurers began to arrive. They were looking for a better and shorter route to the Far East and, specifically, China, than the voyage around Africa. The French established trading posts along the **St. Lawrence River** while the English set up shop around **Hudson Bay**. The high sea road to China and India was never found but the explorers were compensated by teeming fishing grounds and animals covered in valuable fur.

When Europeans first penetrated the inland of Canada, they found it populated by races quite distinct and far more culturally advanced than the primitive Inuit.

These were blood relatives of the peoples encountered by Christopher Columbus when he reached the islands of the Caribbean people he called 'Indians' in the mistaken belief that he had arrived by sailing westward at the fabled Indies reached by Portugese explorers after rounding the African continent a few years before.

Because of the ruddy nature of their complexions and the realization that two vast new continents had been discovered, these races were soon generally termed 'red' Indians. Their migratory background is lost in the mists of time but most modern anthropologists agree that they probably originated deep within the Asian continent and, crossing the land bridge that then existed where the **Bering Strait** flows today, slowly spread from the ice-bound wastes of Alaska throughout the north and south American continents to their very tip in Tierra del Fuego.

The Spanish conquistadors happened upon the finest flowering of these Indian races when they encountered the central American Mayan and Aztec civilizations and, shortly after, the Inca culture of Peru. Even these quite advanced Indian civilizations had yet to discover bronze and iron, yet the essentially stone aged red Indians of North America had, over the tens of thousands of years following their long journey from Asia, developed an intricate and efficient indigenous culture based principally on nomadic hunting and, to a lesser extent, primitive agriculture.

The most advanced Indian tribes inhabiting Canada were those living around the climatically milder areas of the west coast and the St Lawrence River basin. The nations occupying the central and northern area of present day Canada faced much harsher food gathering conditions which tended to preclude permanent settlements and the cultural advances that these settlements bring.

Although all of the Canadian tribes must have been related originally, European explorers finally identified 52 Indian languages or dialects in Canada, all of them stemming from 10 basic linguistic groups. The main group of dialects were those belonging to the **Algonkian** people who occupied an area extending from the Atlantic Ocean to the Rocky Mountains.

The first European exploration was led by **Leif Ericsson**, a Norseman, in about 1000 AD. Sailing from the Viking colony in south Greenland, the Norse certainly coasted parts of Labrador and Newfoundland but the exact location of their reported **Vinland The Good** has never been established and the expedition may have reached as far south as present-day New York State in the United States which is the northernmost place on the North American continent that later settlers discovered wild grape vines growing.

The next known incursion on Canadian shores was by the Englishman, **John Cabot**, who sailed from Bristol and arrived in Canada in 1497. Immigration by European fishermen followed to the Newfoundland Coast and those of America.

In 1534, **Jacques Cartier** of France reached the Gulf of the St. Lawrence River and it is believed, from annotations in his diary, that he named Canada after **Kanata**, an Indian word for 'small settlement.' While he sailed up as far as the place where modern Montreal developed, fishing and fur trading was commenced, for the next 60 years there was no colonization by the French.

Then came **Samuel de Champlain** and, in 1608, he established a settlement on the St. Lawrence River on the site of today's **Quebec** city. Visitors to Quebec should inspect the recently excavated site where Champlain's house was built over an Indian dwelling believed to date from 400 BC. Artifacts removed have included cutlery, cups and bones. The dig is in **Place Royale**, faced by the city's oldest church, and it's here that the birth of French Canada is attributed to have been.

Until his death in 1635, Champlain attempted to promote the fur trade, to see Canada as a French colony, and to explore south and west in his quest to reach China. He discovered **Lake Huron** and **Lake Ontario**, but the western Great Lakes eluded him.

The French faced aggression from the English and from 1618 to 1648 the **Thirty Years War** continued, not only on European soil, but in Canada as well. In 1629, Champlain had surrendered to an English fleet but, under the **Treaty of St. Germain-en-Laye**, Canada was returned to France.

Under the auspices of **Cardinal Richelieu**, the Company of New France, or the Company of One Hundred, was given a monopoly of trade along the St. Lawrence valley. Canadian products could be sent to France duty free. In exchange New France was to receive 300 colonists a year. Company control continued until 1663 when France assumed direct control over its North American possessions.

This was also a period of incredible missionary zeal by the Catholic Church and several Orders arrived to work and convert the Canadian Indians in New France. Greatly influenced were the **Huron tribes**, but because there was bitter war between the Hurons and the **Iroquois nations**, who occupied Lake Ontario's southern shore, the Jesuits became victims of the Iriquois when they almost wiped out the Huron people.

Settlement immediately began to increase and economic activity expanded rapidly. But the colony was dependent economically on the fur trade and, politically and militarily, on France. The colony's future was determined in Europe. The North American continent had become the focus for the animosity between France and England and, in 1763, French North American land, with the exceptions of the **islands** of **Miquelon** and **St. Pierre**, were ceded to Britain.

The French-speaking settlers retained their land, language, religion and laws and, the English made little attempt to attract more of their own people to Canada. But then came the American Revolution in the English colonies to the south where thousands of United Empire Loyalists, who preferred British rule to independence, left their homes and migrated north, mainly into the area of the **Niagara Peninsula**. Their settlements spread east along Lake Ontario's northern shore and the banks of St. Lawrence River.

In 1791, the British Parliament, in recognition of this unsought fait accomplit, passed the Constitutional Act which divided Quebec along the Ottawa River into **Upper** and **Lower Canada**, creating local legislative assemblies in both parts. Upper Canada's first Lieutenant Governor, **Lord Simcoe**, chose the settlement of York, later to be renamed Toronto, as the site of a capital for Upper Canada. This was because it was separated from the infant United States of America by the waters of Lake Ontario.

The legislative system established in these 'two' Canadas parelleled that which had been established by the British in their colony of Nova Scotia.

Internal self government was granted in 1849 after a bumpy transitional period which saw short-lived rebellions occuring in both Upper and Lower Canada in 1837.

Britian's north American colonies of Canada, by then constituting a united Upper and Lower Canada, together with the colonies of Nova Scotia, New Brunswick, Prince Edward island and Newfoundland, grew rapidly. But because of their still relatively scanty resources, these colonies experienced difficulty in providing services such as railways, then spreading westward across the United States of America that would be vitally necessary for the continued development in Canada. Limited markets for their goods, controlled exclusively by the Mother Country, was another constraining factor in the growth of Canadian commerce.

What emerged from these situations was a clear need for the political, economic and cultural unification of the Canadian colonies. But it was not until the emergence of a powerful USA following the Civil War that a convincing argument for this was reached between the colonists and Britain.

On July 1, 1867, the four colonies were united under the terms of the British North America Act. The government of this federation was based on the British Parliamentary system with a Governor General representing the British Crown - and a Parliament consisting of a House of Commons and a senatorial house of review.

The principal architect of Confederation was **Sir John Macdonald** who became Canada's first Prime Minister. While this Federal Government was given dominant power, many subsidiary powers were reserved for the provinces.

In the nearly 125 years that have followed, these powers, principally relating to natural resources and social services, have assumed steadily increasing importance. Following the trend in the USA, Confederation brought in an era of vigourous westward expansion. The vision of a Canada stretching from the Pacific to the Atlantic Oceans became a reality in 1885 with the completion of the Canadian Pacific Railway and new provinces were incorporated into the Dominion of Canada - Manitoba in 1870, British Columbia a year later, Prince Edward Island im 1873 and, finally, Alberta and Saskatchewan in the first years of the 20th century.

The last province to become part of the Canadian Federation was Newfoundland in 1949.

This expansion was not accomplished without the creation of great internal stresses. Rebellions broke out in western Canada in 1870 and again in 1885 but they did not affect the flow of immigrants determined to settle on the vast Canadian prairies.

Tens of thousands of British, Europeans and Americans from south of the 49th parallel migrated to Canada in the years before World War 1. In this late 19th and early 20th century period, Canada profited from a buoyant European and US economy and the capital that any new nation needs to create industries poured into the country. New markets for Canada's natural resources and manufactured goods were also established in this period.

Canada played an important part in this first world conflict, not only through the sacrifices of her sons on the battlefields of France and Flanders, but later in the council

Art Gallery, Toronto

chambers of the Allies in the making of the Peace. Canada's role enhanced its status in the British Commonwealth of Nations and resulted in the attainment of full political autonomy.

Like the rest of the world, Canada suffered greatly during the years of the Great Depression. Many of the nation's industries collapsed and scores of thousands of workers were thrown out of their jobs. It was only after World War II that Canada again began to enjoy its present era of great prosperity.

The Second World War made Canadians aware that the best way to ensure peace was through collective security and Canada, since its creation, has been an active and influential member of the **United Nations**, taking part in all major peace-keeping operations.

For the same reason, Canadians have chosen to join regional military alliances such as the North Atlantic Treaty Organization (NATO) and the North American Air Defence Command.

In these last years of the 20th century, Canadians are very concerned about the future of their nation, particularly in relationship to sovereignty, foreign ownership of resources, national unity and the on-going health of their economy.

Whatever problems they face in the future, the Canadian spirit of restraint, moderation and tolerance, combined with the zeal of pioneers, seems set to continue to characterize the development of Canada.

TORONTO, MORE THAN CAPITAL

The flat plain stretching back from the north west shore of **Lake Ontario** was, for untold centuries, a meeting place of several tribes within the Huron Indian nation.

The present name Toronto is derived from the Huron dialect word meaning just that - **meeting place** - and it was this name that one of the Champlain's adventurous colleagues, **Etiene Brule** gave to the area when he was the first European to visit the lake shores and its hinterland in 1615. The Huron tribesmen were not exactly welcoming, so much so, that it was more than 100 years later before the French colonists managed to establish a trading post and Catholic mission on a site which is now in the western section of the modern city.

Here, in 1750, the French built **Fort Rouille** to protect the small settlement from the warlike Hurons but, during the British-French wars, they razed it to prevent it from falling into English hands.

In the late 1780s, the British bought the site of the former French settlement from the local Indians with payment in standard trade goods and, in 1793, Lieutenant-Governor **John Simcoe**, decided that the settlement was ideal as a capital for the newly formed province of Upper Canada. His decision was dictated by location - because York, the name the British had given their settlement, was reasonably distant from the border with USA and the lake waters and the settlement's harbour were reasonably easy to defend.

In 1797, the small legislature of Upper Canada met for the first time in York. Some 15 years later when the second British-American conflict - the War of 1812 - broke out, the Americans captured the small town and, during their occupation, put the first parliament buildings and the historical archives they contained to the torch.

With the signing of peace between Britain and the US, York was returned to English rule, still a relatively small, administrative settlement and very much a British army garrison town. In 1820, less than 1300 people lived there.

However, in the 1830s, the capital of York began to grow rapidly because of large scale immigration from Britain and Europe to the colony of Upper Canada. Commerce began to be more important than the small city's administrative and military purpose. In 1834, when the population was just below 10,000, the city's name reverted to its original and its centre developed around present day **Yonge Street**, (pronounced Young) which is still the heart of Toronto's business district.

Towards the end of the 19th century, Toronto had become the financial, commercial and industrial centre of the province of Ontario and had also assumed the position of focal point for the expanding railway network. Its position had always dictated its importance as a centre for communications. Stage coach services had commenced from a depot in Yonge Street as early as 1828.

By 1885, the population had topped 120,000 and the city was spreading out over a large area of the plain behind Lake Ontario.

Between 1881 and the outbreak of World War I, Toronto's area increased greatly through a number of annexations. The developed area was divided into several municipalities which caused problems in the delivery of many public utility services. These were not rectified until as late as 1953 when legislation was enacted to combine these urban areas into a federation of municipalities called Metropolitan Toronto. While each of these municipalities retained its autonomy in purely local matters, each elected representatives to a metropolitan council of 25. This Metropolitan Toronto Legislature is responsible for the essential services of water supply, sewerage, public transport, education, health and welfare, law enforcement and similar broad issues throughout the city.

The concept of greater metropolitan Toronto is an example that has been copied in many other great cities of the world since its inception.

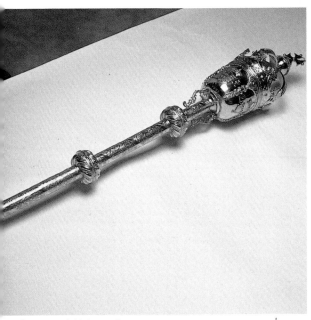

Ceremonial Mace, Ottawa

PART II
Sightseeing

TORONTO

A CINDERELLA CITY

'The city's site was better calculated for a frog pond or a beaver meadow than for the residence of human beings.'

John Graves Simcoe, the man who founded the largest metropolis in Canada, which would later house the biggest subterranean complex of more than 1000 shops and the tallest free-standing structure in the world, the **CN Tower**, had rather a poor opinion of Toronto in 1792.

British author, Charles Dickens, in 1841, was more optomistic when he wrote:

'The country round this town, being very flat, is bare of scenic interest; but the town itself is full of life and motion, bustle, business and improvement.'

Chicago gang lord, Al Capone, in the 1920s, illustrated his lack of even a neo-classical education when he said:

'I don't even know what street Canada is on.'

It is not what street Canada is on, Al. It's what street Toronto is on - and it happens to be the longest in the world, Yonge Street, which runs north from the city's **Queen's Bay** on Lake Ontario to **Rainy River**, a distance of 1896 km!

But walking visitors to Toronto need not be daunted. The city comprises 244 square km of walking discovery - which is enough for one good pair of shoes. Yonge Street passes out of Toronto and continues on through many other Canadian towns before it ends. Although Metro Toronto comprises five cities and one borough, which may mentally increase the footslogger's chagrin, they are nicely linked by good public transport if the leather wears thin.

Despite what Charles Dickens said about the city's flatness - he can't have ventured much further than central downtown - the greater metropolis is slightly hilled and valleyed. This means that in winter, you can cross country ski or don your snow-shoes to explore on foot. Many Torotonians come to work this way.

Known as People City, The City of Cities, Cultural Mosaic and also the City of Lights, Toronto, capital of Ontario Province, was also denigrated as **'Hogtown'** not so very long ago. Few people ventured out of doors after 6 p.m. some 40 years ago and, on Sundays, it was closed - unless one happened to wish to worship at any of its 500 churches.

Such was the influence of the more puritanical of these church congregations that it was regarded as sinful to even window shop at the long-established and marvellous department store, Eaton's, on the day of rest.

But the Cinderella city which had been condemned by the behavior of its most conservative of English-heritage citizens to being dull, unimaginative and even ugly was given a life-saving injection. It was of the vital blood of Italians, Chinese, Greeks, Portugese, Hungarians, Poles, West Indians and many more immigrants who flocked to safety and work following the end of World War II. Now, more than 70 separate national groups, speaking more than 100 languages and dialects, live and work together harmoniously yet individually maintaining their customs and cultures along with their shared national pride.

Another transfusion was a combination of grass seeds and plants. Today, the city is beautifully graced with hundreds of parks, big and small and one of the world's most exciting zoos.

More than 3.6 million people flourish and have fun in this rejuvenated lakeside city of theatre, music, musea, street stalls, restaurants, cabarets, nightclubs and top sporting events. Toronto hums like a well-oiled dynamo.

Into the city has also been transfused a competitive streak that has enabled it to claim so many world firsts - the **CN Tower**, the **Underground City**, the greatest number of television channels in a North American city (there are 40 on the cable system) and the largest concentration of street cleaners of any city of its size on Earth. Above all, Toronto prides itself as being the cleanest great city of the world.

It must take second place somewhere and it is with the biggest theatre community in North America - after New York.

Superman was created by Joe Schuster after his experiences on the **Toronto Star** newspaper, which he changed for his hero's alto-ego, reporter Clark Kent, to The Daily Planet. America's sweetheart of the 1920s' silent silver screen, Mary Pickford, lived in Toronto. **Insulin**, the wonder drug which brought new life and hope to the diabetic sufferers of the world, was discovered at the University of Toronto and author, **Ernest Hemingway**, had one of his first jobs in journalism on the Toronto Star, now Canada's largest circulating newspaper.

Papa Hemingway was among those unimpressed by Toronto because he had to buy chocolate from a bootlegger on the prohibitive Sundays. He should have remained longer.

If time is against you in this lively city, blame Toronto. Standard time's concept was invented here in the 19th century by Sir Sanford Flemming.

However little, or as much you have of it, the time that you give to Toronto will become one of the most fascinating and enjoyable investments of your own, busy life.

Toronto shares the province of which it is capital, **Ontario**, with the national's capital, **Ottawa** which is distinctively different. So if you've seen Ottawa and think Toronto will be similar, think again.

In the broad, beautiful, bold spread of Canada, Toronto is in the far south of the second most easterly of the provinces (discounting Nova Scotia and Newfoundland) next to Quebec province. It is easily accessible from the USA, particularly from Chicago and Detroit and New York via Niagara. **Metropolitan Toronto** is made up of Canada's only borough, that of **East York**, and five cities - Toronto, which has more than nine distinct districts, North York, Scarborough, Etobicoke and the City of York.

On a clear day, so the song says, you can see forever. This is not quite the case from the downtown CN Tower but, with luck, you may glimpse the far-distant prospect of Niagara's mighty falls, some 90 minutes driving time away, or at least urban and delightful wine and orchard country in between. And **Niagara** and **Niagara-On-The-Lake** are two worlds again within themselves.

Let's commence first a voyage, and then your stroll of discovery.

Centre Island

At the Heart of it All

The main north-south street of Toronto, Yonge Street, which extends from Lake Ontario in the south to Highway 401 in the north, begins on the waterfront. Here, or on parallel York Street or from number 17 Union Subway stop, you can make your way to the harbour front and take a ferry or cruise which will put this city of cities in panoramic perspective before you.

Toronto Islands

It is a 10 minute ride by ferry from the harbour front's eastern end next to the **Harbour Castle Westin Hotel**, to Toronto's islands. From the ferry, you gain a super view of the Toronto downtown skyline which is so spectacular, again partly due to the competitive nature of Torontonian developers.

There were three banks which vied to become the city's tallest until a ruling was introduced that no further constructions were to exceed 68 storeys in the city. The fourth bank decided that height was not might and compromised by grinding gold and mixing it in the compound that would make up the windows so that it would be the visually most outstanding from the lake. Indeed, it glistens gold, particularly at sunset. Then, the Bank of Nova Scotia, having taken the city to court over its height limitation and failed, found a loophole in construction specifications. The ceilings of its new building were made a bit more than 15 cm higher than those in the existing bank buildings. This took the bank to a height of 72 standard storeys and the city fathers could do nothing about it. You will see them all from the ferry.

You will also see the CN Tower soaring above them all, the new **Skydome** with its vast, slide-back roof, condominiums, office buildings, the harbour front development, borders of parkland and, on your left as you face the city, the Toronto Island Airport, the nation's third busiest.

The islands actually snuggle into a peninsula's arm which is cut just under its eastern shoulder. The western hook or ham-fist of the peninsula of about 100 hectares is the airport which is interesting for its incredible proximity for commuters to a downtown area and even more incredible to view from the CN Tower. It's rare that observers and diners get to hover so far above aircraft landing and taking off. Originally, the airport was established as an Air Force training base in the Second World War. Now it has three runways and has more than 20,000 takeoffs and landings annually.

From the airport, it is possible to take air sight-seeing flights. If you are arriving from abroad or another province, you will have landed at Peasron International Airport.

> **INFOTIP:** If you have never been to Venice, or are nostalgic for it, keep an eye out for the imported Venetian gondolas which transport up to six people in fine Italian style around Toronto Islands' lagoons.

Toronto's Islands are believed to have begun forming in 600 BC when erosian from **Scarborough Bluff**, the city's major geological feature, was dumped onto a beach by the Niagara current. A sandbar developed, flora grew and west winds shaped the eight-km long peninsula. Native people first populated the islands but, in 1787, sold them for a pittance to the British.

While **John Simcoe** didn't think much of Toronto, he chose it as capital of **Upper Canada** mainly because he saw the islands/peninsula as natural defences for a potential settlement. Later, they became places to picnic, hunt, even observe horse racing. The first ferry service to them started in 1833.

Of the eight islands, Ward, Centre and Hanlan's Point

are of most interest, previously residential but now mainly parklands edged with marinas and jetties harbouring vessels from luxury cruisers to paddle boats.

Centre Island has **Centreville**, a six-hectare amusement park for children including a Canadian village replica, rides, pedal boats and a farm animals zoo. The park is called **Far Enough Farm**. There are formal gardens and a licenced dining room which has a lovely view of the Toronto skyline. There are no vehicles on the islands but bicycles can be hired. (or transported by ferry from the mainland) Walking is also pleasurable. From May to September, you can hire a canoe.

Ferries stop at Ward's Island and Hanlan's Point where there are free tennis courts and the best beaches. There is a train service between Centre Island and Hanlan's Point.

Several companies offer island/harbour boat tours in the May to October high season. These include the steam-powered **Trillium**, a side paddle ferry built in 1910, the only vessel of its kind in North America and leaving at the bottom of Bay Street twice daily from early July to late August.

INFOTIP: You are equally served, minus commentary, and more cheaply on a return trip by regular ferry, particularly if you want to walk around the islands for about two hours (which you can't if you are sailing by cruise boat) If you don't want to walk but take in the spectacular city skyline, opt for late afternoon when the sun invests its gold into those competitive city banks on shore. For schedules of ferries leaving from the bottom end of Bay Street, telephone 947-8193.

Other choices for harbour cruising, including the lagoons of Toronto Islands, are glass-topped sight-seeing boats a la Amsterdam's canal cruises, tall ships, a Victorian-style river boat and chartered yachts. (See Getting Around section) Some companies offer evening and dinner-dance cruises. Most will return via Toronto's busy harbour.

Back on Toronto's shore, you can take a free bus from Union Station to Harbourfront if the ferry/cruise boat of your choice has not returned midway between Parliament Street and Bay Road at Queen's Quay.

Harbourfront

The Harbourfront will be directly in front and to your left if you return from the islands by ferry. This is a 37 hectare development which stretches 2.5 km from the bottom of

York Street to just past Bathurst. It combines open areas with indoor facilities for cultural, recreational and other leisure pursuits as well as shops and offices. More than 4000 events are staged here annually and many are free. Events include activities for the family, performing and visual arts, crafts, marine shows, etc. Canada's largest antique market is here containing more than 100 stalls and shops. Its address is 390, Queen's Quay West, telephone 367-2922.

The sights are linked by a lakeside **Water's Edge Promenade** which runs the length of Harbourfront. In five sections, the complex begins at the eastern end with *York Quay Centre which includes the Power Plant contemporary art gallery, Premiere Dance Theatre, performance centres, crafts studios and Queen's Quay Terminal* which is an exclusive shopping and residential complex. It is open seven days a week and also has international restaurants.

John Quay includes shops, restaurants and the Hotel Admiral. A nautical centre giving sailing instruction and boat rental is at **Maple Leaf Quay**. **Spadina Quay** has shops and Bathurst Quay features Little Norway Park which has sporting fields and a scented garden for the visually disabled.

INFOTIP: If you are travelling in a group of 10 or more, telephone 973-4676, at least two weeks in advance, and you can have a free tour, coach parking and special discount offers from Harbourfront shops and restaurants.

If you continue west along the waterfront you will see a spit of land jutting into the lake. Just before you reach it on **Lake Shore Boulevard**, you will find the Maritime Museum of Upper Canada.

Maritime Museum

Set in Exhibition Place, this museum occupies the historical **Stanley Barracks** which were officers' quarters in 1841. It interprets the rich history of the waterways in central Canada and Toronto's large maritime history as a port for seafaring ships up the St. Lawrence Seaway and lake vessels. An old steam tug lies in dry dock outside the museum and there are relics from sunken ships, models and a captain's bridge from an old pleasure steamer. With a licensed restaurant, the museum is open all year daily except Christmas Day, New Year's Day and Good Friday. Tel: 392-6827.

Also in the grounds of the Canadian National Exhibition is another museum.

Ontario Place Marina

Canadian National Exhibition

You can't miss this old building. It is a huge ediface more than 100 years old although there have been additions over the century. It has everything that a **World Fair** should, including displays of books, animals, crafts and cars. Outdoor bands provide entertainment. A ferris wheel, a roller coaster and other amusements delight children. It's a combination of gaudiness, modern technology and history that attracts thousands of visitors.

Hockey Hall of Fame and Museum

In this museum, the oldest North American sports trophy, the **Stanley Cup** is exhibited. Hockey fans will see sticks wielded by past and present stars of the sport and also skates, jumpers, goalie masks and other memorabilia of ice hockey, which is Canada's national sport. Tel: 595-1345.

Ontario Place

Scadding Cabin

Built by a pioneer, **John Scadding**, this log cabin is Toronto's oldest house. After it was moved to Exhibition Place in 1879, it was maintained as an example of the home of an early 18th century Ontario pioneer. It is open all day during the Canadian National Exhibition, in June, Labour Day and Wednesday to Sunday afternoons and evenings weekly.

That spit of land mentioned off Lake Shore Boulevard West is **Ontario Place**, a world-famous cultural, entertainment and leisure complex reclaimed from Lake Ontario into three islands. It is at 955 Lakeshore Boulevard.

Ontario Place

Built on the islands and over the lake, straddled by futuristic steel legs, this complex is a child's dream which has a playground, an exciting wilderness adventure ride, a children's village, bumper boats, a marina, a World War II destroyer, HMCS Haida, an outdoor Forum concert stage and a Cinesphere. The latter is a huge, domed auditorium in which 70 mm IMAX films are projected onto a curved screen six storeys high with devastating realism. Future Pod is a showcase of the latest high tech developments and Ontario North now is the northern province's theme pavilion.

One stage at the western end has a waterfall for a curtain and the flume waterslide with its simulated rapids and tunnels is another popular attraction of Ontario Place. With a dozen restaurants, the 40 hectare complex also has beer gardens and parklands for picnicking. It is open from mid-May to October from 10 a.m. to 1 a.m. Tel: 965-7711. There is an admission charge and extra for amusement rides and slides.

Baseball Hall of Fame and Museum

Recently incorporated into Ontario Place, this museum is open from 10 a.m. to 9 p.m. daily and includes displays representing more than 150 years of baseball history in Canada. Visitors can try pitching and batting and there is a theatre showing baseball films.

Fort York

After leaving Ontario Place, you are a short walking distance from this early 19th century fortification which you will find on Garrison Road, off Fleet Street, just west of Bathurst Street.

The drama of the War of 1812 between Britain and the United States is re-enacted through tours, military demonstrations and displays at this most important historical site. Built by the British in 1793 when the town was called York, the fort was almost obliterated at the end of the 1812 conflict. But afterwards it was rapidly reconstructed. It comprises stone, brick and eight authentic log buildings. If you visit Toronto in summer, you will see soldiers wearing 19th century English military uniforms, marching, drilling and firing their muskets.

Open year round between 9.30 a.m. and 5 p.m. There is an admission charge.

If you now get back to Lake Shore Boulevard and continue west with **Sunnyside Beach** (nice for strolling and picnicking) on your left, you will reach High Park on your right on Parkside Drive between Lake Shore Boulevard and Bloor Street West.

High Park

This park is rambling in some areas, neatly manicured in others. Set by **Grenadier Pond**, which was named after the British Redcoats who paraded its frozen surface in winter, the park and pond now offer skating in winter and boating and fishing in summer. Included are sports fields, outdoor sculptures and a small zoo which exhibits native birds, deer, bison and yaks. High Park is also home to Colborne Lodge.

Colborne Lodge

A main claim to fame of this interesting and picturesque Regency-style home built by an early Toronto architect **John G. Howard** is that it includes what is believed to be Upper Canada's first indoor toilet. It also has a resident ghost, the architect's wife who is said to wander past the lovely original antiques in the house at night. It was built in 1837 by Howard who was also the city surveyor, engineer and an artist. There are demonstrations of domestic life in the 19th century given each day.

Colborne Lodge is open year round with the exception of Christmas and New Year's Days and Good Friday.

Now return to the shore of Lake Ontario.

Skydome, Baseball

> **INFOTIP:** If you are into swimming or yachting in summer, you have 17 marinas and seven swimming pools along the Metropolitan Toronto shore of Lake Ontario from which to choose.

Before entering the hustle and bustle of the city proper, continue your exploration of the waterfront by heading back east along Lake Shore Boulevard.

Redpath Sugar Museum

On Queen's Quay, at number 95, is this museum which contains a collection of memorabilia on the Canadian sugar industry and also the pioneering family, the Redpaths. Machinery and other equipment used in early sugar production is shown, along with a film, Raising Cane, to which admission is free. Group tours are by appointment. Tel: 366-3561.

Now, continue for some distance along the waterfront until you reach Woodbine Beach Park and Beaches Park.

Beaches Park

If by now you are tired of walking, you could catch an east-bound **Queen streetcar** (tram) and alight anywhere between **Greenwood Race Track** and **Neville Park** which is at the end of the lines.

At the Greenwood Race Track, thoroughbred and harness racing is held year round.

Beaches Park is a former affluent and charming old residential neighbourhood become parkland. While the lake fronting it is not good for swimming - in fact swimming is prohibitied here - this is a lovely area to walk through or cycle along bike tracks. You can suntan, picnic and rent sailboards. There is a swimming pool in **Woodbine Beach Park** which is adjacent to Beaches Park.

Just north of Beaches Park the main road becomes Kingston Road and about 5 km from the beaches are the Scarborough Bluffs.

Scarborough Bluffs

Go down Brimley Road from Kingston Road to find these 90 metre high limestone cliffs which have been surrounded by parkland. The odd-shaped bluffs display sediment layers which indicate five different glacial periods in their geological history. Entwined with paths, the park also has mooring space by the lake for vessels of many types.

You are now actually in one of Metro Toronto's cities, that of Scarborough. From the bluffs you will see the most spectacular view in Ontario with the exception of that from the CN Tower. It will include **Niagara Falls**, too if it is a good day. Should you wish to charter a boat for salmon fishing, do it from here.

Also, the bluffs include a hotel estate, the Guild Inn. It has an historical architecture display and a collection of facades, panels and gates from about 60 of Toronto's most important and venerable buildings. Tel: 261-3331.

You are now, on foot or by vehicle, almost half way to Toronto's zoo, famous not only throughout the North American continent, but the world.

Toronto Zoo

Off Kingston Road, the zoo is north along Meadowvale Road. It is also accessible by public bus. Take number 86A from Kennedy Subway Station which is east of the central Bloor-Yonge Station in the heart of the city. It is more than 25 kilometres from the downtown area.

The zoo, which is *open year-round*, is as much a botanical garden with its horticultural collection valued at more than $5 million. It has eight tropical pavilions comprising the **Indoor Zoo** for more than 240 exotic exhibits. The Toronto Zoo was opened in 1974. It is so large - 121 hectares of walking area and about 160 hectares of valley - that it is worth at least a day's visit. The valleys are accessible by monorail which operates year round. This system gives visitors a chance to see herds and species roaming freely across six major reserves.

The areas have been transformed into African savannah, Malaysian rain forest and climatic and topographical representations of Australia, Eurasia, the Polar regions and the Americas. These are in a series of indoor and outdoor habitats and huge free-form pavilions. The climate-controlled pavilions include recreated swamps for Florida alligators, Malaysian monkeys and there are ponds for the Canadian beaver. More than 4000 animals, reptiles and birds live in environments as close to their natural homes as possible.

In winter a Zoo Ski programme enables visitors to cross-country ski between animal exhibits. Equipment and lessons are available. Other facilities include restaurants - they say the world's biggest MacDonald's is here - picnic tables, Zoomobile, camel and pony rides, guided tours and wheelchair and stroller hire.

With the exception of Christmas Day, Toronto Zoo is open daily between 9.30 a.m. and 7 p.m. in summer and 9.30 p.m. and 4.30 p.m. in winter.

> **INFOTIP:** Do not be tempted to send the kids off to the zoo alone. Without an adult, no child under 12 is admitted.

Now, reorientate yourself back on the waterfront just below Union Subway Station for an exploration of the main attractions of the downtown area of the City of Toronto.

Look up. It demonates the skyline - the fabulous CN Tower.

CN Tower

Built to withstand the force of a colliding DC10 jetliner, the **Canadian National** or **CN Tower** as it universally known, has become Toronto's symbol, the tallest free-standing structure on earth. It is north of Queen's Quay between Yonge Street and Spadina Avenue, off the Gardiner Expressway at 301 Front Street West.

Measuring 553.33 metres in height, it can be ascended by four glass-faced elevators in a thrilling 58 seconds. Descending is at the rate of a free-falling parachutist.

At the base is a **Tour Of The Universe** which is a realistic simulation of space flight on board CN Tower's Canadian Airline's Hermes class IV space shuttle which blasts you into the 21st century. The 'flight' is to Jupiter in the year 2017, the 50th anniversary of Neil Armstrong's first moon walk. The simulator straps in 40 passengers for a 50 minute orientation through videos and holograms. The cabin sways and jolts realistically. Interesting inter-galactic characters await visitors.

> **INFOTIP:** This journey, a sensual treat, is not for the faint-hearted - seriously. Medical warnings are posted and if you have a heart condition, do not attempt it.

At the 346 metre level is Toronto's top nightclub, literally. Sparkles has good music and is the best place to view the city at night. Admission is free after evening dining at the **Top Of Toronto**. This restaurant, at 350 metres is the world's highest and largest revolving restaurant where Continental cuisine can be enjoyed during an aerial tour spanning up to 160 kilometres of Toronto and Ontario. The restaurant makes one revolution each 72 minutes. While there are taller towers in the world, these others have supporting cables for stability. This functional communications tower also has a public observation deck. From it a special elevator takes visitors to the **Space Deck** at 447 metres.

The tower also includes a pool-side lounge and souvenir shop. There is access for the disabled at the Tower's Lake Shore entrance. For information and group bookings, Tel: 360-8500. Reservations for dining and nightclub, 362-5411.

Skydome

From CN Tower, you will see the spectacular Skydome at 277 Front Street West. This vast stadium is Canada's first multi-purpose sporting, entertainment, conference and trade show facility with a fully retractable roof and the first such facility in the world to house a top class hotel. Located beside Toronto's Convention Centre, Skydome holds trade and consumer shows, concerts and sports events. It includes more than 15,000 square metres of exhibit space, 55,000 fixed seats and up to 70,000 fans can attend rock concerts. For details of events, Tel: 963-3515.

Old City Hall

Still on Front Street West, slightly east, at 100 is the **Royal York Hotel**, which is a Toronto institution, being the largest hotel in the British Commonwealth, with 1600 rooms. Opened to serve the public by Canadian Pacific Railways in 1929, it has been temporary home to a list of royals, heads of State and celebrities that would take pages to include, from Queen Elizabeth II to movie star Raquel Welch. With seven different dining rooms and as many bars, it's an old-style, gracious place to stop for snack, meal or drink. The hotel is also linked with the underground shopping city.

The hotel's side entrance faces York Street which is just a short block east of University Avenue.

Toronto is laid out on a grid system which is easy to negotiate on foot but because the greater metropolis is large, you would be wise, if short of time, to utilize the superior public transport system - bus, underground railway or subway and trolley car (tram) Do not use the latter word as you will not be understood.

Most streets run north-south and east-west and, basically, downtown is from east-west-running Front Street to Bloor Street (also east-west) in the north and bordered by Spadina Avenue (to the west) and Jarvis (east) Street which extend from south to north. As previously stated, Yonge Street is the south-north spine, closely followed by parallel University Avenue - where you are now.

> **INFOTIP:** If you are looking for garments at all prices, check out Spadina Avenue, Toronto's fashion district.

Wherever you are in Toronto, know the direction in which you are headed. Street names change to east and west off University Avenue.

Curve into University Avenue and head north (or take the subway from Union Subway station to the St. Andrew stop if you are tired) Union Station is just across from the Royal York Hotel and is the main terminal for inter-provincial trains and also for those connecting with New York and the United States rail network. Turn left into King Street West and at number 260 you will see the baroque **Royal Alexandra Theatre**. Go here for hit plays from London and New York, including the best from Broadway. Many productions include big name stars and occasionally Torontonians present good plays here as well.

The Royal Alex is very close to **Roy Thomson Hall** which is the home of the Toronto Symphony Orchestra, the Mendelssohn Choir and a favoured venue of visiting performers. The hall seats 2800 and is distinctively designed.

From here, proceed east along King Street until reaching York Street, then turn north along York until you reach Adelaide Street West. On the corner at the Exchange Tower, number 2, First Canadian Place, is the Toronto Stock Exchange.

Toronto Stock Exchange

Open year round Monday to Friday, the Stock Exchange is the largest public securities market in Canada. It is set in the heart of the city's financial district, has a visitors' centre and, if you are interested to see how more than $100 million of stocks change hands in one of the world's most technically-progressive trading floors, you can take a free, guided tour. There are also interesting audio-visual presentations.

Now, get back on University Avenue and continue north until you reach its intersection with Queen Street West, just near Osgoode Subway station. At number 160 is Campbell House.

Campbell House

This is the beautifully-restored brick residence of Sir William Campbell who was **Chief Justice** of **Upper Canada** from 1825 to 1829. This mansion includes a miniature model of the **Town of York** as it was in 1825.

Campbell House is open from late May to Thanksgiving Day every day. The rest of the year, it is open Monday to Friday. Tel: 597-0227.

You will be tempted to continue along Queen Street West because, by now, you will have discovered it is Toronto's rejoinder to London's Soho.

If it's handicrafts in the making or the trendiest of fashions possibly created by an undiscovered avant garde designer that you seek, you should find it here, along with street entertainers, way-out art, antiques and interesting bistros. This is a street of character and characters.

Satisfied? Turn back along Queen Street West, heading east, cross University Avenue and soon, on your left, you will see **Nathan Phillips Square** which is dominated by City Hall.

City Hall

The square is still regarded as the city's real meeting place where rock concerts, brass band performances and various other events are held. This is a place to people-watch. They may be on political soap boxes, suntanning in summer or skating on a frozen pool in winter.

City Hall, at the square's northern end is twin-towered and was completed in 1965.

The building is closed weekends and holidays but tours can be taken Monday to Friday after advance booking. Tel: 392-7341.

From City Hall head west along Armoury Street, which will return you to University Avenue. Turn right and go north until you reach Dundas Street West. Now, turn left into Dundas for two blocks. There are two points of interest here, The Grange and the marvellous Art Gallery of Ontario.

Art Gallery of Ontario

If you want more and more of Moore, this is the gallery to visit for its enormous **Henry Moore** sculpture exhibits. Here, are more than 600 of his works. One of the top three galleries and fine arts museums in the nation, this fine arts museum demands a lot of time because of its diversity of displays. It houses more than 10,000 works from Old Masters to the latest in contemporary styles. There is also a wing devoted to a fascinating Canadian collection, including the famed Canadian Group of Seven.

Check the newspapers for visiting exhibitions. Most of them are marvellous. You can have refreshments in the cafeteria here and also browse through a good bookshop which sells reproductions. Films are shown and lectures given.

The gallery is open all year daily, except Mondays. The hours are 11 a.m. to 5.30 p.m. with the exception of Wednesday when the gallery remains open until 9 p.m. Admission is charged except on Wednesday evening. Tel: 977-0414. Your admission ticket will take you to The Grange which can be entered via the gallery's basement, next to the cafeteria.

The Grange

This elegant Georgian house was originally owned by a prominent Toronto family until it was bequeathed to the Art Gallery. Matthew Arnold, on entering this gentleman's residence, circa 1830, wrote that he had discovered *'nothing so pleasant and so home-like in all our travels.'*

The Grange is staffed by period-costumed guides and is open all year, daily, except Mondays, Christmas Day and New Year's Day. It remains open to 9 p.m. on Wednesdays. Tel: 977-0414, ext. 237.

New City Hall

Chinatown

You might want to deviate here and continue west along Dundas Street because this is the biggest of Toronto's five districts where the Chinese live, work and prepare terrific food. The area is very popular with visitors who find that in addition to many restaurants, there are also authentic Chinese shops selling all manner of goods as well.

If you stroll west until you reach Spadina Avenue then turn left into it (south) you will soon happen across China Court.

China Court

This is the relatively new focal point of Chinatown and is a conglomeration of Chinese gardens and authentic pagodas which were imported from Hong Kong and set up by craftsmen. They stand amidst more restaurants and Chinese shops.

If you want to follow the fashions south along Spadina Avenue, continue. Otherwise, retrace your steps back to University Avenue along Dundas Street.

Along University Avenue, you will see the sausage or hot dog vendors in greatest concentration. Munching on one as you stroll or sit on a street bench is recommended.

Proceeding north along University Avenue, you will pass the new Mt. Sinai Hospital on your left, the Children's Hospital on your right, followed by Toronto General Hospital. If this section of your Toronto walk seems too daunting, take the subway one stop from St. Patrick to Queen's Park, which is on College Street. University Avenue now becomes the circular Queen's Park Crescent, which encircles the Parliament building dead ahead and Queen's Park behind them. Take the left fork.

> **INFOTIP:** If you are looking for an Italian eatery, you will find one in Little Italy which is roughly bordered by College Street and St. Clair Avenue.

Parliament Building

The Provincial Parliament Building is an imposing one of granite and pink sandstone. Built in the late 1800s as the forum for Ontario's politicians, it is welcoming of visitors who can walk its marbled halls or listen to debate in the Legislative Chamber. It is open from late May to Labour Day, daily, from September to May on weekdays, and when the House is in session from October to December and from February to June (approximately).

The solid **Ontario Government Buildings** are to the right of the Provincial Parliament on Queen's Park Crescent East.

Facing north, you will see the Sigmund Samuel Canadiana Building at 14 Queen's Park Crescent West.

Sigmund Samuel Building

This is a must for lovers of antiques. There are silver coins, medals, maps, currency, paintings, glassware and displays of room settings as they were in Canada's early days, along with period furniture.

Open year round daily, this Canadiana exhibition is closed Christmas Day and New Year's Day.

Ukrainian Festival

University of Toronto

Just a little further west is the University of Toronto where about 60,000 students attend. The campus is a little scattered but you will find around a green playing field various architectural styles including the 1859 **University College** (Romanesque,) and **Hart House**, built in the Gothic style. In English, Spanish, French and German, hour-long walking tours of the campus are conducted free, Monday to Friday from June to the end of August.

If you are attending a performance advertized for **Convocation Hall**, you will find it here. It is used for concerts when not required by the university.

Continue past Queen's Park and the road heading north becomes Queen's Park Road. On your left is the McLaughlin Planetarium.

McLaughlin Planetarium

Here you can recline in special seats to enjoy a laser-light concert and see the wonders of the Heavens reproduced. They are projected on to the huge dome of the planetarium. Several of these star shows change yearly. Programmes last 45 minutes and, in the planetarium's Astrocentre, there are audio-visual presentations, hands-on exhibits, a solar telescope which allows visitors to look at real sun flares and other astronomy equipment.

The planetarium is open all year daily except for Mondays, Christmas Day and New Year's Day.
Tel: 586-5750.

> **INFOTIP:** This is a very popular venue so get there early. The subway stop is Museum.

Royal Ontario Museum

This museum (known affectionately as **ROM**) is adjacent to the planetarium and, with 6 million treasures highlighting science, art and the evolution of civilization, is Canada's largest public museum. Its collection includes fossils, art and archaeological exhibits and its display of Chinese textiles and crafts is considered one of the best outside China. There are also displays reflecting the glories of the ancient Egyptian, Greek, Etruscan and Roman civilizations.

Popular exhibits include replicas of a huge Ming tomb, a Buddhist temple, an Islamic house and an Egyptian tomb, complete with mummy.

Nathan Philips Square

There are also rooms devoted to the study of mammals and the dinosaurs. The history of trade from ancient caravan routes in Asia to today's world trade between east and west is graphically depicted.

There are facilities for film shows, dance performances, lectures, craft demonstrations, shopping and eating.

The museum is open year-round daily between 10 a.m. and 6 p.m. and on Tuesday and Thursday to 8 p.m. It is closed on Christmas Day and New Year's Day. Tel: 586-5549.

INFOTIP: Admission is free on Thursday after 4.30 p.m. unless there is a special ticketed exhibition. If you visit the museum on the same day as the planetarium, you will receive a discount on admission to the planetarium.

On the right of Queen's Park Road, heading north, is the George R. Gardiner Museum of Ceramic Art at number 111.

George R. Gardiner Museum _____

Opposite ROM, this relatively new museum has a rich collection of ceramics from pre-Columbia pottery, Italian majolica and English Delaware to a large collection of 18th century European porcelain. This includes Italian comedy figures and scent bottles. Exhibits date back more than 2000 years.

The museum is open daily year-round from 10 a.m. to 5 p.m. except for Mondays and national holidays. It has a gift shop. Tel: 593-9300.

Your are now at the intersection of Avenue Road (the continuation of Queen's Park Road) and Bloor Street. Bloor Street is renowned for its movie theatres, up-market restaurants and high-fashion boutiques. First, turn left along Bloor Street West for the Museum of the History of Medicine.

Ray Thomson Hall

Museum of the History of Medicine _____

At number 288, this museum is Canada's major medical history museum, housed in the **Academy of Medicine**. The collection traces 5000 years of medical practice and health care. It includes special exhibits and the **Drake Childcare Collection**.

Open weekdays all year except public holidays, admisssion to the museum is free. Tel: 922-0564.

Now, turn around and retrace your way back along Bloor to Avenue Road.

You can continue walking along Avenue Road or take the subway from St. George to Dupont station for Casa Lona which is at 1, Austin Terrace off Devonport Road, which branches to the left off Avenue Road.

Casa Loma _____

You will love it or hate it - one man's dream - a 98-room medieaval-style castle! Soldier, financier, industrialist and incurable romantic, **Sir Henry Pellat**, spent $3 million in 1911 to build his dream home. He studied old world castles, brought glass, panelling and marble from Europe, walnut and oak from prime North American forests, teak from Asia and engaged stone masons from Scotland to build the massive wall that surrounds the 2.5 hectare property.

Before World War I, royalty was entertained in the greatest of luxury with the most ingenious inventions of the era. But the upkeep of Casa Loma became too much for Sir Henry and in the early 1920s the City of Toronto took the castle as payment for back taxes.

Visitors can explore the Conservatory with its bronze doors, Peacock Alley, a replica of the historical hallway in Windsor Castle, and the Great Hall, with its ceilings nearly 20 metres high.

Three artisans took two years to complete the French oak panelling in the Napolean Drawing Room and the library had accommodation to shelve 100,000 books.

Sir Henry and his Lady lived in the greatest of luxury in their private suites and, from his study, Sir Henry could escape to privacy via a secret staircase. There is an excellent view from the battlements and a 250 metre tunnel leads to towered stables of mahogany and Spanish tiles, where fine horses and elegant carriages were once housed.

Casa Loma has a cafeteria, gift shop and is accessible to the disabled. Admission in charged and the proceeds used by the **Kiwanis Club** of **West Toronto** to assist youth, senior citizens and the intellectually handicapped.

Spadina House

At 285, Spadina Road, this house crowns the magnificent estate of financier, **James Austin**. It contains elegant furnishings and fine art enjoyed from 1866 by Austin and three generations of his family.

The gardens are lovingly landscaped and guided tours are conducted all year, daily, except Christmas, Boxing and New Year's Days and Good Friday. On Sundays and holidays, it is open afternoons only.

Return to Bloor Street South via Spadina Road or the subway and get off at either Spadina or Bay stations. Otherwise, retrace your steps south along Avenue Road, where at its intersection with Cumberland Street, Yorkville begins.

Yorkville

Here, and extending south to Bloor Street, and east to Yonge Street, the former town of Yorkville has been wonderfully restored. Yorkville became a village in 1853. Today's Yorkville is full of historical homes and chi chi restaurants and boutiques. It fell into disrepair and disrepute as a hippy hangout in the 1960s. But the hippy element was ousted by affluent yuppies and the city have restored most of the interesting and gracious old homes.

It is an area to stroll, shop, people-watch, dine and to enjoy the nightlife.

> **INFOTIP:** If your feet give out, a novel way to get around is by cycle rickshaw. You will also find them in the Yonge Street and waterfront areas offering tours from historical to shopping.

When you reach Yonge Street, turn north for the Metropolitan Toronto Library.

Metropolitan Toronto Library

At 789 Yonge Street, this is Canada's largest public reference library housed in a stunning building. Architect **Raymond Moriyamas** brought warmth, colour, light and spaciousness to what, in other cities, is usually a staid institution. There are 48 km of shelves which accommodate 1 million books which include a comprehensive Canadian collection, and a unique collection on **Sir Arthur Connan Doyle's** immortal **Sherlock Holmes**.

INFOTIP: If you think the children might be bored at this institution, drop them off at the Boys and Girls' House which is part of the library. It encloses a marvellous collection of childrens books from the 14th century onwards.

With the exception of closing on Sundays between May and October, the library is open every day except public holidays. Tel: 393-7196.

Head south along Yonge Street until its intersection with Charles Street. Turn left here and continue to the inter-section with Jarvis Street.

Having Fun?

Metropolitan Toronto Police Museum _____

At this corner is the Metropolitan Police Museum which is located in the Police Headquarters building. The museum contains very interesting displays and documents related to the most famous crimes committed in Toronto.

The museum is open weekday year round. It stays open on Thursday and Friday evenings. Afternoons only Saturday and Sunday.

Continue south along Jarvis Street where, opposite McClear Place, are the Allan Gardens.

Allan Gardens _____

Set in a square bordered by Jarvis, Sherbourne, Carlton and Gerrard Streets, this park is an oasis in the downtown area. It is a place to stop for a picnic on its lawns, beneath its trees and to visit a huge greenhouse. More than 70 years old, the greenhouse contains tropical and semi-tropical trees, flowering creepers and plants. The greenhouse is open all year, daily.

To get back to Yonge Street, head south on Jarvis Street and turn right at Gerrard Street.

Eaton Centre

> **INFOTIP:** If you are interested in an authentic Indian meal, turn in the opposite direction in Gerrard Street and make your way east as far as the intersection of Gerrard and Coxwell Avenue in the Borough of East York - the only borough in the city. It is a fair distance but here you will discover Toronto's Little India.

Assuming that curry didn't tempt you, you are now proceeding south on Yonge Street until you reach Dundas Street East. Deviate east again along Dundas until you reach Bond Street and Mackenzie House at 82.

Mackenzie House

This was the mid-Victorian home and print shop of Toronto's first mayor, **William Lyon Mackenzie**. He was also the leader of the ill-fated rebellion of 1837. Mackenzie was a vital character and so are the mementos of his life. Daily, except in December, afternoon tea is served. In December, with the exception of Christmas Day, the house recreates a Victorian-era Christmas with mulled cider, cranberry punch and oatmeal cookies (biscuits) available to visitors.

With the exceptions, also, of New Year's Day and Good Friday, Mackenzie House is open daily, year round.

On the opposite side of Yonge, on its intersection with Dundas Street West, is the fabulous Eaton Centre.

Eaton Centre

One of Canada's three retailing giants, the Eaton store chain in Toronto is the company's flagship. The Eaton Centre links with another large competitor, Simpsons, and is part of the vast, subterranean shopping city which we will be exploring soon. The centre has 300 indoor shops and service outlets on four levels. Stretching beneath a glass-domed galleria which extends down Yonge Street from Dundas to Queen Streets until it meets Simpsons, the Eaton Centre is a movie-goers nightmare. Who could choose from 21 cinemas?

If you have emerged from Eatons at Simpsons, you have missed Massey Hall. It is at the corner of Shuter Street (which runs off Yonge,) and Victoria Street, which runs parallel to Yonge.

Massey Hall

While this 1894-built concert hall is not weathering time too well, its acoustics are among the best in North America. It has seen many great performers, including Caruso, and continues to be a popular venue for performances of all types.

Toronto's First Post Office

Had you continued south down Jarvis Street from Allan Gardens, you would have come across Toronto's first Post Office, which is on the corner of Adelaide Street East, at 260. With the **Bank of Upper Canada**, the post office is the only remaining building on its original site in the Town of York. The bank and the post office have been designated National Historic Sites. Restored to its original state circa 1830s, the post office represents the British postal period before 1851. A postmaster in period dress provides philatelic and contemporary postal services and, for a small fee, you can address your mail with quill and seal it with wax before posting.

The post office is open seven days a week between 10 a.m. and 4 p.m. Tel: 865-1833.

Opposite the post office is the tranquil St. James Park.

Continue down Jarvis Street until you reach Front Street where the St. Lawrence Centre for the Arts is situated at number 27.

St. Lawrence Centre

This home base for Canadian actors includes a modern theatre for classic and Canadian drama and a hall in which international-standard chamber and solo music recitals are conducted. It was the public gathering place of 19th century Toronto and is still one of the city's finest historical buildings.

At that time, there was a fruit, flower and vegetable market behind it and, although the building in which the market was held no longer exists, the trading still continues. Behind the site, across Front Street, is a large building which was **Toronto's first City Hall** in 1844. It has been part of the market since 1890. If you want to pack a picnic lunch, here is where you will find bread, olives, cheese, meats, fruit and everything else you may need. The market is actually on Jarvis Street between Front and King Streets.

It is open all year but the North Market functions on Saturday only. The South Market is open Tuesday to Saturday.

O'Keefe Centre

Next door to the St. Lawrence Centre is the O'Keefe Centre which, with 3200 seats, is a large, modern concert hall. It is home to the **National Ballet** of Canada which, yearly, presents an exciting dance season. In addition to ballet and opera, the centre also hosts various international and Canadian performances. It has a restaurant for before and after theatre dining. Tel: 872-2262.

Market Gallery

While you are on Front Street, check out the Market Gallery at number 95 (Front Street East) This is the city's official exhibition facility and displays paintings, photographs, maps, documents and artifacts from the city's art collections and municipal archives. Tel: 392-7604.

You are now just a short distance from Union Station down from which your tour of Toronto, via the harbour, began. If you go into the basement of the Royal York Hotel at 100 Front Street West, you can start a subterranean exploration which is likely to last all day.

Bellvue House

Art Gallery, Tornoto

BENEATH THE STREETS

If you are visiting Toronto in winter, you will not need to worry about braving the snow when shopping, because Toronto has the largest underground city in the world. It has 4.8 km of tunnels and, from the Royal York Hotel or Union Station, it stretches six city blocks to the *Toronto Dominion Centre, First Canadian Place, The Sheraton Centre, Simpsons Department Store* and the *Eaton Centre*, ending in the north of downtown at Atrium on Bay, which is on West Dundas Street and accessible from Dundas subway station.

The plans for the underground city began to develop in the early 1960s, essentially to reduce the number of

pedestrians walking above ground. Then, it was decided to give Torontonians opportunity to shop and dine as well as walk. The city fathers' dreams for their city materialized in 1977 when the Eaton Centre opened. The complex includes 1000 stores, banks, restaurants, medical suites, movie theatres and even a nightclub.

The underground city is served by seven subway stations.

Regardless of the climatic conditions outside, the temperature literally downtown is carefully controlled for comfort.

It would not be practical for us to duplicate the attractions you have already seen above ground in the central city area, but it might be interesting to, perhaps, finish your excursion to the north by returning south under the ground, maybe beginning at the Eaton Centre and seeing daylight again at Union Station.

BEYOND DOWNTOWN

Out for the Day

With the exception of the Metropolitan Toronto Zoo and the Bluffs in Scarborough City, so far the tour of Toronto has been confined to the central area of the city. But there are many more things to see in the greater metropolis. They are not withing walking distance and they are scattered.

Ontario Science Centre

Located at 770 Don Mills Road in the **City of North York**, north-east of downtown and about 10 km from Union Station, the Ontario Science Centre can be reached from the Yonge Street subway station. Travel north to Eglinton station, then change to the Eglinton East bus. Alight at Don Mills Road. Alternatively, take the Bloor Street subway

Science North Sudbury

east to the Pape station, then catch the Don Mills bus. Get off at St. Dennis Drive in front of the centre.

The centre is a hands-on museum which challenges the senses as well as the intellect, showing that technology and science are absorbing parts of everyone's lives. You can touch, pull and push without being told to desist. The centre is set in a futuristic building and has 700 exhibits. You can simulate a moon landing, be separated from your shadow and have your hair stand on end when you touch 500,000 volts - safely! There is a *Hall of Technology*, a *Disorientation Chamber* and the setting itself, is well worth a visit. Kids of all ages love it.

Facilities include a licensed restaurant, two cafeterias, a gift shop (good for books and educational presents,) and wheelchairs and children's strollers can be hired.

It is open year round except Christmas Day from 10 a.m. to 6 p.m. daily and three more hours on Friday evenings. Admission is charged. Tel: 429-0193.

You could combine a visit to the Ontario Science Centre by returning via the Borough of East York, where, at 67 Pottery Road is the Todmorden Mills historical site.

Todmorden Mills _____

Returning south, get off the subway at Broadview station and take any bus to Pottery Road. From there it is just a short walk down Pottery Road Hill to find the mills.

This is an important 19th century mill site by the waters of the Don River. Two pre-Confederation houses have been restored along with a former brewery which now houses various historical exhibits. The old Don railway station includes a train museum.

The museum is open from 11 a.m. to 5 p.m.on weekends and holidays and from 10 a.m. to 5 p.m. Tuesday to Friday. It is closed Monday. Admission is charged. Tel: 425-2250.

Gibson House _____

Just more than 15 km north of Union Station is Gibson House which you could visit on your general exploration of the central Toronto area if you continued north along Yonge Street into the **City of North York**. But it may be more convenient to make this a separate excursion. You can reach Gibson House by subway. The nearest station is North York Centre, from where you just have to walk north to 5172 Yonge Street.

Gibson House is the superbly-restored 1850 mansion built by **David Gibson** who was a local politician, land surveyor and a staunch supporter of **William Lyon Mackenzie** in the 1837 rebellion. You may have learned about the patriotic pair when visiting Mackenzie House earlier. The brick home offers daily demonstrations of pioneer crafts and cooking. Occasionally, you may see preserves being prepared from the products of the Gibson House garden.

It is open from 9.30 a.m. to 5 p.m. weekdays and on weekends and holidays from noon to 5 p.m. It is closed Christmas, Boxing and New Years Days and Good Fridays. Admission is charged. Tel: 225-0146.

Black Creek Pioneer Village _____

This village is more than 20 km north-west of Union Station, about 30 minutes driving time, but accessible by Steeles West 60 bus from Finch subway station or the Jane 25 bus from Jane subway station. Both stations can be reached from Union. The village is on the corner of Steeles Avenue West and Jane Street, **City of North York**.

The Black Creek Pioneer Village is a re-creation of a rural pioneer community of pre-Confederation days in Ontario. The 'villagers' wear period costumes as they work at pioneer crafts and go about their daily business of grinding flour in the mill and shoeing horses, among other tasks.

There are also cooking and baking demonstrations, the results of which can be bought by visitors, a herb garden, a toy museum and wood carving is also explained. At certain times of the year, including the **July 1 Canada Day**, there are special celebrations. In summer, children can participate in 19th century games on the Village Green and there is an annual pioneer festival in September. This is one of the best autumn fairs in the Toronto area and features the making of **Mennonite-style quilts**. (The Mennonites were, historically, an extreme puritanical Canadian Christian sect) There are cooking demonstrations too.

The pioneer village complex is open from mid-March to December daily. Admission is charged. Some tour complanies include it in their itineraries. Tel: 736-1733.

Sudbury Downs

Canada's Wonderland _____

This $C152 million answer to the glitzy, children's fantasy theme parks of the USA is north again from Black Creek Pioneer Village. You could combine the two in one day but the attractions of both are likely to run you out of time.

The 150 hectare park is situated on the east side of Highway 400 between Rutherford Road and Major Mackenzie Drive. You can reach it by public transport from either York Mills or Yorkdale subway stations then by **GO buses** which depart for the entertainment complex about every 30 minutes.

There are seven distinct themes in the park - *International Street, International Festival, Mediaeval Faire, the Grand World Exposition of 1890, Smurf's Forest, White Water Canyon* and *Hanna Barbera Land* which is dedicated to the creators of the TV carton series *The Flinstones*.

Entertainment includes more than 34 rides, (try Canada's first stand-up roller coaster), live shows, top entertainment at the Kingswood Music Theatre and shops and restaurants.

The park is open from May 7 to October 2, from 10 a.m. to 8 p.m. weekdays and 10 a.m. to 10 p.m. on weekends. Tel: 832-2205.

Sunshine Beach Water Park

If you have wheels, you can go south from Canada's Wonderland on Highway 400 until you reach Steeles Avenue West (where the Black Creek Pioneer Village is) then turn west until you reach Indian Line or Highway 427. The **Claireville Conservation Park** and **Reservoir** will be on your right and, below it, Canada's first water theme park.

It is more than 25 km as the crow flies from Union Station. This big park offers wonderful fun for children between June and September. There are slides galore and a wave pool.

Open 10 a.m. to 8 p.m. in the season, there is an admission charge. Tel: 794-0468.

About 3 km almost due south of the park is the Woodbine Race Track.

Woodbine Race Track

Off Indian Line, on Rexdale Boulevard at its intersection with Highway 27, is the venue where North America's oldest stakes horse race, **The Queen's Plate**, is held annually. This is the biggest and most renowned race track in Canada. Woodbine's Spring-Summer Thoroughbred meetings run to October 30. Up till August, meetings are held from Thursday to Sunday from 1.30 p.m. and, on Wednesdays, 4 p.m. September Wednesday races begin at 3 p.m.

There are buses from Islington subway station and special rates apply on these buses in the racing season.

The Upper Canada Brewing Company _____

A win at the race track is good excuse to treat yourself to some of Toronto's own beer. The Upper Canada Brewing Company at 2, Atlantic Avenue is Toronto's only cottage brewery. Tour groups or individuals can be conducted through the operation from Monday to Saturday.

You will see lager, dark ale and light beer being brewed in the old fashioned way without additives or chemical preservatives. Sampling, of course. Tel: 534-9281.

There are so many day trips which one could take from downtown Toronto into the province of Ontario that it would be impossible to list them with their features in this *InfoGuide*. But within an hour, one can be away rambling through farm and forest landscapes and quiet villages such as Alton with its waterfalls and **Brampton**, the **Flower City** with its numerous nurseries, **Great War Flying Museum** and five-storey high indoor white water slides.

You can explore unspoiled villages and lakelands but because the choices of destination are so great, it would be advizable to pick up some literature from Ontario Tourism Information Centre, Eaton Centre, 220 Yonge Street (level 1) open 10 a.m. to 9 p.m. weekdays, Saturday 9.30 a.m. to 6 p.m. Closed Sunday.

Also, you can gain info at 900 Bay Street, 1st floor, Macdonald's Block, open weekdays 8.30 a.m. to 4.30 p.m. year round. Tel: 965-4008.

If you prefer to speak French, call 965-3448.

Niagara on the Lake

SIDE TRIPPING

A Day or Two or More

Even if only curiosity to see why, each year, more than 15 million honeymooners alone are attracted to what must be the world's Bedroom Capital, you must visit **Niagara Falls**. It is only 90 minutes drive south of Toronto. (You head west and Lake Ontario's shore curves to the south) There are several tour operators who will take you there for a day tour or one that extends. (See Tours in the Practical A-Z section of this InfoGuide)

If you have never visited Africa, stop off on the way to Niagara at the African Lion Safari which is equidistant in an hour from Toronto, London (Ontario) or Niagara Falls.

Niagara Falls

African Lion Safari

This is a drive-through wildlife park where exotic animals roam free. One gains a package admission ticket to explore six large game reserves, a cruise aboard the **African Queen**, a scenic railway trip on the **Nature Boy train,** a flying demonstration by birds of prey, a show presented by parrots and a performance at the **Animal Amphitheatre**.

The park, located between the cities of Hamilton and Cambridge, on Safari Road between Highway 6 and Highway 8, also has special entertainment, rides and wet and dry play areas for children. Naturally, shows and rides are subject to weather conditions in the season which goes from April to October.

Open weekdays 10 a.m. to 4.30 p.m. and weekends and holidays, 10 a.m. to 5 p.m. Admission is charged. Tel: (519) 623-2620.

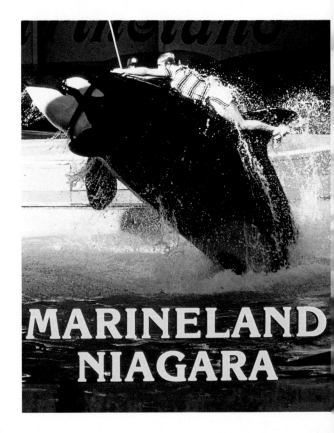

NIAGARA FALLS

A Wonder of Nature's World

Niagara Falls is accessible by several daily trains from Union Station and from the bus terminal at 610, Bay Street in Toronto. Grey Lines operates a good value, daily, return tour to Niagara Falls including lunch, Niagara-On-The-Lake and a winery visit.

Should you be travelling by road, you will pass through long sections of urbanzation, by the industrial city of Hamilton and then get into orchard, flower and wine producing country. Orchards and vineyards welcome visitors to taste and buy. If you are motoring independently, look for signs directing you to them from the highway.

> **INFOTIP:** For the first time in her life, one author of this InfoGuide discovered a bottle at one winery under the label Cooking Wine. Take her tip - and believe it!

You should see, later, the picturesque haven that is **Niagara-On-The-Lake**, a world apart from The Falls and the spectacular, massive tumbling of the **Niagara River** plunging to its fumy destiny in **Lake Ontario**.

In geological terms, Niagara's mighty falls are in their infancy. The Niagara River came into being about 10,000 years ago when the recession of the **Great Continental** ice sheet at the end of the **Glacial Epoch** exposed the escarpment of dolomite rock over which the river thunders.

The falls are wearing away this rock at the rate, in recent times at least, of about 1.5 metres annually. The gorge is now about 11.2 km long and, if the recession towards **Lake Erie** continues at this rate, the gorge will join with the lake in about 25,000 years and cause the total drainage of it. So see it before this happens.

It is not known for certain who was the first European to see this awesome sight, but the Frenchman **La Salle**, wintered by the falls in 1678. The French built a fort at Niagara in 1725 and it became an important military trading post. **Fort Niagara** which is on the American side of the river, remained a regular post for the US Army until 1945.

The falls have been the scene for many death-defying exploits since one, **Sam Patch**, leaped into the river in 1829, went over the falls and lived to tell the tale. Since then, several men and women have successfully plunged over the **Canadian Horseshoe Falls** in barrels and other containers. In 1859, and again, in 1860, the French aerial wire artist, **Charles Blondin**, performed amazing feats on a tightrope stretched across the gorge just below the falls.

More recently, a seven-year-old boy in swimming costume and light life vest fell into the river running at 48 km per hour above the falls. He emerged alive at the foamy, rocky base to be rescued by a **Maid of the Mist Tourist Boat**, a vessel which you can join yourself.

If you are arriving by bus or private vehicle, you will come into Niagara Falls by the Niagara Parkway South well after crossing Welland Canal. This is a good way to begin your tour of Niagara Falls because once you get up into the hilly streets which run west, you may wonder why you have come.

The streets branching off Niagara Parkway south are filled with the most incredible, bad-taste establishments you could possibly imagine. Yet, if you are in a holiday mood and out for a bit of zany fun, they could well take your fancy. They'll certainly give you a laugh.

One street in, on Portage Road, which runs parallel with Niagara Parkway South, you can visit Marineland.

Marineland

You will not yet have realized that Niagara Falls has become victim to every kind of entertainment to produce tourist dollars that is possible to devize. One of the more interesting and value for money attractions is Marineland which is home to performing *killer whales weighing up to seven tonnes, dolphins, comedy sea lion shows* (the claim is that this is the world's largest troup,) and other creatures such as *ducks, deer* and *bears*.

There are also amusement rides including Canada's largest steel roller coaster, **Dragon Mountain**.

At 7657, Portage Road, the park opens in summer from 9 a.m. to 6 p.m. and off-season between 10 a.m. and 4 p.m. Attractions vary according to the season. Admission is charged. Tel: 356-9565.

On the parkway, just before you reach the point where you can observe the **Horseshoe Falls** and **Goat Island**, so named because these animals once roamed it, is the **Niagara Park's Greenhouse** where there is a year-round floral display. Admission is free.

Next north are the scenic tunnels through which, for an admission charge, one can view the falls from a subterranean vantage point. As in the Maid of the Mist boats, you will probably get very wet, despite the raincoats that are standard gear for visitors.

Almost diagonally opposite the tunnels but well elevated is the Minolta Tower.

Minolta Tower

The Minolta Tower can be reached by continuing along Portage Road and it is quite a climb to Oakes Drive. Now, you will have more than an inkling of the commercialization of the area rising up from the falls - motels everywhere, a building with tired Rapunzel towers, restaurants, fast food and souvenir shops, old fashioned buses and newer vehicles inscribed Honeymoon Tours. You can take the Niagara Park's Incline Railway from the falls to reach the tower which is at **6732 Oakes Drive**.

The Minolta Tower was the first to be built to command a breathtaking view of Niagara Falls. There are three open observation floors and an enclosed observation area with windows designed for photography. The tower is nearly 165 metres above the Horseshoe Falls and about 185 metres above **Niagara Gorge**. As you stare down, you will see, by day, the perpetual rainbow curving up out of the rising mists from the magnificent falls.

Centre Island Ferry

There are Top of the Rainbow dining rooms and, in winter, the tower transforms into what is claimed to be the world's tallest candle for the November Festival of Lights, a celebration which runs to February annually. The tower features a **Waltzing Waters** spectacle of 972 water jets dancing, changing colour and swirling to music, a view which is free to night diners from May to October.

Other facilities include a gift shop and Canada's so-claimed largest reptile exhibit. Tel: 356-1501.

The bus terminal is not far from here but before you reach it, if you look up, you will see the Skylon Tower which is at 5200 Robinson Street.

Skylon Tower

The tower faces the **American** or **Bridal Falls** and is almost 240 metres above the Niagara River. Also a participant in the winter **Festival of Lights**, the Skylon Tower features buffet breakfasts, lunches and dinners in its Summit Suite and has a revolving restaurant at the top. Tel: 356-2651.

Just up the road at 6170 Buchanan Avenue, is the Niagara Falls IMAX Theatre.

Harbour Front

IMAX Theatre

This theatre features Niagara: *Miracles, Myths and Magic*. More than seven storeys high, this, the largest movie screen in Canada, enables visitors to experience the larger-than-life vista of the raging waters and a thrilling ride over the falls in a death-defying stunt. There is six-track channel sound to accompany the visuals. The theatre resembles a giant pyramid and, in summer, shows are presented daily on the hour. There is a gift shop and a snack bar.

North again, on River Road, down from Clifton Hill is the place to embark to experience the full might of Niagara Falls. The Maid of the Mist powerful, diesel engined sightseeing boats leave from the Canadian side of the Niagara River after one has descended many steps or taken a funicular ride down the face of the gorge.

INFOTIP: You will be provided with heavy raincoat and hat as you will get very wet but also take a plastic bag in which to protect your camera otherwise it will be sprayed, or possibly saturated with water. Also, if your time at Niagara Falls is limited, make this trip your first priority. Queues to get on the boats are usually very long.

Maid of the Mist

Maid of the Mist tourist boats take passengers up the **Niagara Gorge** for a distance then turn to pass very closely the **American Falls, Goat Island** and then bucks as it enters the cascades of the mighty **Canadian Horseshoe Falls**. You will experience the launch pitching and rolling and may even wonder if its engines are strong enough to return you to the shore. They are.

The Maid of the Mist fleet of boats operate from mid May to October. No reservations. First in line, first aboard.

Agawa Canyon

The Canadian Falls crash down nearly 55 metres at the rate of nearly 20,000 cubic metres of water each second. At night, the falls are illuminated by coloured searchlights, creating added splendour and romance when seen from above.

> **INFOTIP:** Do not dismiss a winter visit to Niagara Falls. The Festival of Light will entertain by night but the Niagara River is also inspiring as weird, natural ice sculptures form along its banks, creating further visual excitement.

Clifton Hill, probably the most garish of all Niagara Falls' streets, slopes up from where the Maid of the Mist funicular departs down the face of the gorge.

Clifton Hill

Walk Clifton Hill just to be vastly amused by motel signs advertizing rotating waterbeds, heart-shaped spas, in-house adult movies - and special family rates! Along and fanning out from this bawdy bedroom belt, you will discover the **House of Frankenstein, Tussaud's Waxworks** and a **Movieland Wax Museum, The Haunted House, Castle Dracula** and amusement galleries offering rides, thrills and spills.

You can become a star by recording the music hit of your choice at the Super Star Recording Studio. **The Guinness Museum** of **World Records** is also on Clifton Hill, one block from the falls.

For information on the seven days a week activities on Clifton Hill (including the city's 'hottest' nightclub, Rumours) Tel. 356-2299.

Maple Leaf Village

Behind Clifton Hill, off Highway 420, is the Maple Leaf Village and **Amusement Park**. The village has managed to acquire the greatest collection of **Elvis Presley** memorabilia outside of Gracelands and Hollywood. They are exhibited on the second level and include Elvis' cars, furniture from Graceland and his Hollywood homes, jewellery, clothing, personal items and photographs.

On the top level, fans of the American television show **That's Incredible** will find a museum on the world's wonders based on the series.

North again, off River Road, between Queen and Bridge Streets is the Niagara Falls Canada Visitor and Convention Bureau at 4610, Ontario Avenue. Tel: 356-6061.

On River Road at 5651 is the Niagara Falls Museum.

Niagara Falls Museum

Open year round daily, this museum has a collection of the containers in which people have gone over the falls. There are other curiosities which have nothing to do with the falls at all, including a collection of Egyptian mummies!

Just beyond, almost opposite Whirlpool Bridge which spans the Niagara River to the USA, is the *Canadian National Railway Station*.

> **INFOTIP:** You can cross by four bridges but, be warned, you must hold a valid American visa gained before you leave your own country.

Still heading north, you can take the **Great Gorge** trip by boat and then the **Spanish Aerocar**, in which you are suspended in a basket across the swirling waters of the Niagara River as it rushes relentlessly towards Lake Ontario.

A little further north again, you will find the **Niagara Parks' School of Horiculture Floral Clock** and then, the Whirlpool Golf Course. Here, you can cross-country ski in winter.

A good tour is conducted in London-style buses by Double Deck Bus Tours, 3957, Bossert Road.
Tel: 295-3051.

Another tour is offered by Niagara Parks Commission, which operates from mid-May to mid-October. Tickets for this tour are sold at booths near the falls. Tel: 356-7633.

This, excellent-value, tour includes the *Table Rock Scenic Tunnels, Maid of the Mist* boat tour, *Great Gorge* trip and the *Niagara Museum* plus the *Spanish Aerocar* ride. Land transport is by London-style bus. Included in the cost is a meal.

Stops are also made at free attractions including the **Niagara Parks Greenhouse, School of Horticulture**, the **floral clock** and **Queenston Heights Park**.

An intrreresting way to experience the 'tallest, widest, biggest, longest, most exciting ride in Niagara' is by *Niagara Helicopters, River Road*. Tel: 357-5672.

The flights follow the Niagara River, cross the rapids and the American Falls, then bank over the spectacular Horseshoe Falls.

> **INFOTIP:** It is not advized that you forget your camera but, if you do, this company will lend you one.

The first official honeymooner at Niagara Falls is believed to have been *Emperor Napoleon Bonaparte's* brother. Should you be in the same situation, you will find honeymoon packages a way of life with Niagara hotels and motels.

Along the Niagara Parkway, which becomes River Road, you will also find lovely, grassed and treed picnic spots and ample parking areas if you are driving. A wonderful thing about Canada is that in picnic areas there are free-standing picnic tables and chairs to help you enjoy your al fresco meals and, incredibly, nobody steals them. In most other countries, these facilities are cemented into the ground.

In addition to the winter **Festival of Lights**, Niagara hosts a **blossom festival** in spring and a *peach festival* in summer while in autumn the **Grape** and **Wine festival** pays tribute to the surrounding wine-producing areas.

There are also innumerable theme parks in and around Niagara Falls, including Whitewater at 2430 Lundy's Lane. Tel: 357-3380 and Niagara Go Karts at 7104, Kinsmen Court. Tel: 356-9030.

INFOTIP: You will not dare to go over the falls in a barrel just to get a souvenir shot to show the folks at home. But such a picture can be simulated by photographers operating out of the Skylon Tower, Clifton Hill area and Maple Leaf Village. Tel: 356-8033.

Now, make your way north along the picturesque River Road through scenic Queenston to lovely Niagara-On-The-Lake.

The drive from Niagara Falls to Niagara-On-The-Lake is absolutely beautiful. It is a distance of 20 km and a charming way to experience it is to walk if you are fit and have time or to ride a bicycle. There are hire firms in Niagara Falls. There are a couple of wineries on River Road. This road follows the Niagara River very closely. It is thickly treed and the parklands on your left are glorious with varied tree species. The School of Horticulture is well worth visiting.

Fort George

A couple of kilometres before you reach Lake Ontario, you'll come to **Fort George National Historic Park**. The defence of the Niagara Frontier was strategically important to the survival of Upper Canada, particularly during the British-American War of 1812. The frontier was vulnerable to American attack from across the Niagara River and so it was guarded by a series of military structures in the area of Niagara-On-The-Lake.

Of these, Fort George was the principal bastion and was involved in continuous battles with Unites States armies during that war. A combined land and naval bombardment and an assault by the Americans levelled the fort in May 1813. The Americans occupied the ruins and re-built the defences but 18 months later abandoned the fort again to the British.

After the war, other fortifications became more important and the British ceased to use Fort George as a military post in the mid-1820s. Today, the fort shows the installations as they were from 1796 to 1813. The defences consist of six small earthern bastions connected by cedar picketting. The whole complex is surrounded by a dry ditch. The only original building is the stone powder magazine constructed in 1796.

Actors in period costume portray everyday life in a British military post of nearly two centuries ago and a self-guided walking tour introduces visitors to all of the features of this park. Fort George opens daily from mid-May to October 31 but it can be visited by arrangement on weekdays, with the exception of public holidays, from November 1 to mid-May. Admission is charged.

Niagara-On-The-Lake

It is as if those who planned and developed the ritz and glitz surrounding one of the world's natural wonders have been shamed by powers who be - those who have decided to maintain this section of land leading to Lake Ontario as it was in the late 19th century.

Homes, shops and public buildings have been lovingly restored and, in this region, you can experience some of the best of Canada's bed and breakfast accommodation in English style cottages, guest houses and country inns.

Niagara-On-The-Lake has a lovely golf course facing the lake and you can cross country ski across it in winter.

Formerly *Ontario's capital in the 1890s*, now the village is one of the best preserved small towns in the nation. All the streets are attractive but Main Street particularly so. Stroll it to absorb the feel of affluent Canadian life in the 19th century. Flowers dance from window boxes. Hanging baskets add more greenery to the gracious avenue.

Niagara-On-The-Lake **Historical Museum** at 43, Castlereagh Street is said to be Ontario's oldest. *It is open daily*. But perhaps Niagara-On-The-Lake's greatest claim to fame is the Shaw Festival, of international as well as Canadian renown.

Whitewater rafting, Ottawa River

The Shaw Festival

Theatrical works by the famed English playwrite **George Bernard Shaw** and other dramatic writers are performed in this yearly festival at Niagara-On-The-Lake's theatres, principally the Festival Theatre, from April to October. Entertainment is continuous at the three main theatres and one can almost forget that they are in Canada and believe this could be England.

> **INFOTIP:** Should you be hearing impaired, you can obtain a phonic ear receiver in all of the Shaw Festival theatres. There is a small charge. Arrange to get one when you book tickets.

The peninsula is intersected by many roads and if you have time to stay in the general area, you can criss-cross it and hardly ever end up on the same route. Those staying in Niagara Falls could return there via Highway 55, deviating to the charming town of **St. Catherines** through which you will have passed on your way to the falls. It has a nice winery. Otherwise, continue through St. Catherines back to Toronto.

One of the most successful wineries is on Highway 55, just out of Niagara-On-The-Lake. Although **Hillebrand Estate Winery** is only a few years old, the traditions of its wine makers go back more than 250 years to the German Rhine Valley.

Winery tours are conducted year-round, daily at 11 a.m., 1 p.m., 3 p.m. and 5 p.m. It includes a walking tour, audio-visual presentation and complimentary tasting of some interesting varietal wines. Tel: 468-7123.

If it is during the season and you have your own wheels, you could deviate at Hamilton and continue to **Cambridge** and **Kitchener**. Follow Highway 8, west through Kitchener and take Highway 7/8 west again to Stratford where the famed Stratford Festival is conducted every year.

Stratford Festival

Pretty Stratford set by the **Avon River** is deliberately landscaped to adopt the atmosphere found in England, the home of William Shakespeare. In three theatres, Shakespeare's works and those of other renowned playwrites are performed from June to October. Tickets run out quickly.

To book from Toronto, call (free) 363-4471, or write to Stratford Festival Box Office, PO Box 520, Stratford, Ontario N5A 6V2.

Off to Ottawa

As the national capital, which shares the same province of Ontario with Toronto, Ottawa cannot be ignored as a possible side trip. It is 400 km north-east of Toronto, less than one hour's flight from *Pearson International Airport* and accessible at reasonable price by bus and train from Toronto.

Ottawa, should, of course, be ideally seen in as much depth as Toronto but for the purposes of a side trip, it is suffice to say that Canada's capital, a combination of old and new, French and English, is set on the southern bank of the **Ottawa River** and very much worth investigating.

It is separated into east and west by the Dutch-like **Rideau Canal** on which commuters skate to work in winter (when there is a marvellous festival,) and which also features horse racing on ice.

With its connections with The Netherlands, *Ottawa is Canada's tulip capital.* Its Parliament Building has changes of the guard with the soldiers crowned by British-like busbies that could be straight out of Buckingham Palace, London.

Ottawa's art galleries and museum include the futuristic granite and glass **Canadian National Gallery** and the **National Aviation Museum** are among the nation's most exciting. Also across the **Alexandra Bridge** in the province of Quebec at Hull, the **Museum of Civilization** ranks as one of the most absorbing centres of culture and learning in the world. Don't miss it.

Ottawa is not a huge city, but it is a pretty one, full of constrasting architecture. Its cultural awareness is paramount and, from Ottawa, with its many fine parks and cycling tracks, one can white-water river raft, boat, fish and hike.

For those who would like a short experience of the Canadian capital, detailed information can be gained from the Ottawa Tourist Office, 14, Metcalfe St., Ottawa, Ontario. Tel: 992-5473.

RCMP Musical Ride, Ottawa

PART III
Accommodation

Toronto Island

HOTELS AND CAMPING SITES

GENERAL NOTES

The Ontario Provincial Government blurb warns the visitor: *'Seeing Ontario can become very habit-forming.'* This is why you have, following, such a range of accommodations in Toronto, Niagara Falls, Stratford and the capital of Ottawa, from which to choose.

In the whole of Ontario, a voluntary accommodation rating system has been created by the province's Tourism Authority. They have been listed alphabetically rather than by conventional star rating.

Top Toronto hotels are a dream, spacious, comfortable, well-serviced and the older properties have fascinating histories as well. Some of the city's outstanding restaurants are incorporated in them.

Checkout times vary but are generally from 10 a.m. to noon with late-departing guests able to maintain their room or suite longer for an additional special rate, if there are vacancies.

Bed and Breakfast Accommodation

In addition to the above accommodations, Toronto offers clean and homely bed and breakfast accommodation. There are more than 20 homes which welcome guests in the Metropolitan Bed and Breakfast Reistry of Toronto, 77, Lowther Ave. Tel: 964-2566 or 928 2833. The registry organization is a member of the Metropolitan Toronto Convention and Visitors Association. It publishes a list of establishments and will handle bookings.

Camping

Glen Rouge Park, 365, Bay St. Tel: 382-8092. 117 sites, 87 of which have electricity and water. Toilets and showers.

Indian Line Tourist Camp Ground, Downsview (Take Highway 427 north to Finch Ave., then 1 km west.) Tel: 678-1233.
225 sites, 186 with electricity and water. Toilets and showers.

Milton Heights Camp Ground, Campbellville Rd., Milton. Tel: 878-6781. 450 sites, 200 with electricity and water of which 106 have toilets and showers.

Accommodation

Toronto West, KOA Campbellville. Tel: 854-2495.
100 sites, 72 with electricity and water. Toilets and showers.

Niagara Falls

Campark Resorts, 9387, Lundy's Lane. Tel: 358-3873.
100 sites, all with water, 82 with electricity and 44 with personal showers. Toilets and showers.

Green Oaks Camp Ground, 8223, Stanley Ave. Tel: 358-8005,
30 sites, 10 with electricity, water and personal showers. Toilets and showers.
Niagara Falls KOA, 8625, Lundy's Lane.
Tel: 354-6472.
340 sites, 283 with electricity aand water and 70 with personal showers. Toilets and showers.
Orchard Grove Tent & Trailer Park, 8123, Lundy's Lane.
Tel: 358-9883. 400 sites, 300 with electricity and water, 170 with personal showers. Toilets and showers.

Yogi Bear Jellystone Park Camp-Resort, 8676,
Oakwood Dr.
Tel: 354-1432. 305 sites, 207 with electricity, 97 with water. Toilets and showers.

Niagara-On-The-Lake

Shalimar Lake, on Niagara River Parkway, 10 km north of Niagara Falls. Tel: 262-4895. 350 sites, 258 with electricity and water, 198 with personal showers. Toilets and showers.

Legend
S - Babysitting
AC - Air Conditionings
G - Golf
ISP - Indoor Swimming Pool
OSW - Outdoor Swimming Pool
SA - Sauna
T - Tennis
TV - Television
U - Conference Facilities
WP - Whirlpool (Spa)
CC - Credit Cards
B - Bar
R - Restaurant

Dining in Ottawa

TORONTO

BEST WESTERN
CARLTON PLACE HOTEL
Hwy 27 N & Dixon Rd
Rexdale M9W 6H5
Tel. (416) 675 1234
AC, ISP, SA, TV, U, WP, CC

BRISTOL PLACE HOTEL
950 Dixon Rd
Rexdale M9W 5N4
Tel. (416) 675 9444
AC, ISP, SA, TV, U, CC

CAMBRIDGE MOTOR HOTEL
600 Dixon Rd
Toronto M9W 1J1
Tel. (416) 249 7671
AC, OSP, TV, U, CC

CARA INN
6257 Airport Road
Toronto L4V 1E4
Tel. (416) 678 1400
AC, G, ISP, SA, TV, U,
WP, CC

SKYDOME HOTEL
45 Peter Street Sth
Toronto
Tel. (416) 361 1400
AC, G, ISP, S, TV, U,
WP, CC

CARLTON INN HOTEL
30 Carlton Street
Toronto M5B 2E9
Tel. (416) 977 6655
AC, ISP, SA, TV, U, R, CC

CHIMO HOTEL
7095 Woodbine Avenue
Markham L3R 1A3
Tel. (416) 474 0444
AC, ISP, SA, TV, U, R,
B, WP, CC

THE DELTA CHELSEA INN
33 Gerrard Street W
Toronto M5G 1Z4
AC, ISP, SA, TV, U, WP,
CC, R, B

Rideau Canal, Ottawa

THE DELTA MEADOWVALE INN
6750 Mississauga Rd
Mississauga L5N 2L3
Tel. (416) 821 1981
AC, G, ISP, SA, T, TV,
U, WP, R, B, CC

EXECUTIVE MOTOR HOTEL
621 King Street W
Toronto M5V 1M5
Tel. (416) 362 7441
AC, TV, U, B, CC

FOUR SEASONS HOTEL
21 Avenue Rd
Toronto M5R 2G1
Tel. (416) 964 0411
AC, OSP, OP, SA, TV, U,
WP, CC, R, B

THE GUILD INN
201 Guildwood Park
Scarborough M1E 1P6
Tel. (416) 261 3331
AC, G, OSP, T, R, B,
TV, U, CC

THE HARBOUR CASTLE WESTIN
1 Harbour Square
Toronto M5J 1A6
Tel. (416) 869 1600
AC, ISP, SA, TV, U, R,
B, WP, CC

JOURNEY'S END MOTELS
25 Finch Avenue E
Downsview M3N 1X1
Tel. (416) 736 4700
AC, G, TV, R, B, CC

JOURNEY'S END MOTELS
111Lombard Street
Toronto M5C 1M2
Tel. (416) 367 5555
AC, TV, CC

L'HOTEL
225 Front Street W
Toronto M5V 2X3
Tel. (416) 597 1400
AC, ISP, SA, TV, U, R,
B, WP, CC

NEW LIDO MOTEL
4674 Kingston Rd
Toronto M1E 2P9
Tel. (416) 282 5768
AC, OSP, TV, CC

NEW PLAZA MOTEL
4584 Kingston Road
Scarborough M1E 2PA
Tel. (416) 284 9966
AC, TV, CC

**QUALITY INN
ESSEX PARK HOTEL**
300 Jarvis Street
Toronto M5B 2C5
Tel. (416) 977 4823
AC, TV, U, R, B, CC

**SEAHORSE MOTEL,
FRIENDSHIP INN**
2095 Lake Shore Blvd
Toronto M8V 1A1
Tel. (416) 255 4433
AC, OSP, T, TV, U, CC

METRO INN
2121 Kingston Road
Toronto M1N 1T5
Tel. (416) 267 1141
AC, G, TV, U, R, B, CC

MOTEL 27
650 Evans Avenue
Toronto M8W 2W6
Tel. (416) 255 3481
AC, G, TV, CC

**THE SHERATON CENTRE
HOTEL & TOWERS**
123 Queen Street W
Toronto M5H 2M9
Tel. (416) 361 1000
AC, ISP, OSP, SA, B, R,
TV, U, WP, CC

SHERATON PARKWAY HOTEL
600 Hwy 7 East
Richmond Hill L4B 1B2
Tel. (416) 881 2121
AC, G, ISP, OSP, SA, B,
R, T, TV, U, WP, CC

Accommodation

SHORE BREEZE MOTEL LTD
2175 Lake Shore Blvd W
Toronto M8V 1A1
Tel. (416) 251 9613
AC, OSP, TV, CC

SUTTON PLACE HOTEL
Cnr Bay & Wellesley St W
Toronto M5S 2A2
Tel. (416) 924 9221
AC, ISP, SA, TV, U, R,
B, CC

TORONTO GATEWAY INN
4694 Kingston Road
Scarborough M1E 2P9
Tel. (416) 284 9922
AC, ISP, TV, WP, CC

VISCOUNT HOTEL
55 Hallcrown Place
Willowdale M2J 4R1
Tel. (416) 493 7000
AC, G, ISP, SA, TV, R,
B, U, WP, CC

THE WESTBURY HOTEL
475 Yonge Street
Toronto M4Y 1X7
Tel. (416) 924 0611
AC, TV, U, R, B, CC

THE WINDSOR ARMS HOTEL
22 St Thomas Street
Toronto M5S 2B9
Tel. (416) 979 2341
AC, TV, R, B, CC

AMERICANA MOTEL
2757 Kingston Rd
Toronto M1M 1M8
Tel. (416) 261 7191
AC, G, TV, CC

BEACH MOTEL
2138 Lake Shore Blvd W
Toronto M8V 1A1
Tel. (416) 259 3296
AC, TV, CC

**THE SKYLINE
TORONTO AIRPORT**
655 Dixon Rd
Rexdale M9W 1J4
Tel. (416) 244 1711
AC, G, ISP, SA, T, B,
R, TV, U, WP, CC

**THE SKYLINE
TRIUMPH HOTEL**
2737 Keele Street
Downsview M3M 2E9
Tel. (416) 633 2000
AC, G, ISP, SA, R, B,
TV, U, CC

BOND PLACE HOTEL
65 Dundas Street E
Toronto M5B 2G8
Tel. (416) 362 6061
AC, TV, U, R, CC

CARLINGVIEW AIRPORT INN
221 Carlingview Drive
Toronto M9W 5E8
Tel. (416) 675 3303
AC, OSP, TV, U, R, B, CC

HERITAGE INN SANTARO
385 Rexdale Blvd
Toronto M9W 1R9
Tel. (416)742 5510
AC, G, OSP, TV, U, R,
B, CC

**HILTON INTERNATIONAL
TORONTO**
145 Richmond Street W
Toronto M5H 3M6
Tel. (416) 869 3456
AC, ISP, OSP, SA, R, B,
TV, U, WP, CC

HOLIDAY INN
1250 Eglinton Avenue
Don Mills M3C 1J3
Tel. (416) 449 4111
AC, G, ISP, OSP, SA, R,
B, TV, U, WP, CC

EMERALD ISLE MOTEL
8700 Yonge Street
Thornhill L4C 5M2
Tel. (416) 889 5411
AC, G, OSP, TV, CC

HILLCREST MOTEL
2143 Lake Shore Blvd W
Toronto M8V 1A1
Tel. (416) 255 7711
AC, G, TV, CC

HOLIDAY INN
22 Metropolitan Rd
Scarborough M1R 2T6
Tel. (416) 293 8171
AC, G, ISP, OSP, SA, R,
B, TV, U, WP, CC

**HOTEL ADMIRAL
AT HARBOURFRONT**
249 Queen's Quay W
Toronto M5J 2N5
Tel. (416) 364 5444
AC, OSP, TV, U, WP, R,
B, CC

HOTEL IBIS
240 Jarvis Street
Toronto M5B 2B8
AC, TV, U, R, B, CC

IDLEWOOD INN
4212 Kingston Rd
Toronto M1E 2M6
Tel. (416) 282 2335
AC, G, OSP, SA,
TV, WP, CC

INN ON THE LAKE
1926 Lake Shore Blvd
Toronto M6S 1A1
Tel. (416) 766 4392
AC, B, TV, U, B, R, CC

LAKE EDGE MOTEL
2077 Lake Shore Blvd W
Toronto M8V 1A1
Tel. (416) 259 5441
AC, OSP, TV, CC

LAKESHORE INN
2000 Lake Shore Blvd W
Toronto M6S 1A2
Tel. (416) 763 4521
AC, ISP, SA, R, B, TV,
U, WP, CC

MAPLE LEAF MOTEL
4540 Kingston Rd
Toronto M1E 2N8
Tel.(416) 282 6257
AC, G, TV, CC

**MARRIOTT HOTEL
TORONTO AIRPORT**
901 Dixon Rd
Rexdale M9W 1J5
Tel. (416) 674 9400
AC, ISP, SA, TV, U, R,
B, WP, CC

NOVOTEL TORONTO CENTRE
45 The Esplanade
Toronto M5E 1W2
Tel. (416) 360 8900
AC, ISP, SA, TV, U, R,
B, WP, CC

**RAMADA HOTEL
DON VALLEY**
185 Yorkland Blvd
Toronto M2J 4R2
Tel. (416) 493 9000
AC, ISP, SA, TV, U, R,
B, CC

RAMADA INN
1677 Wilson Avenue
Toronto M3L 1A5
Tel. (416) 249 8171
AC, G, ISP, SA, TV, R,
B, U, WP

**RELAX PLAZA HOTEL
NORTH YORK**
50 Norfinch Drive
Downsview M3N 1X1
Tel. (416) 663 9500
AC, G, ISP, TV, U, R,
B, WP, CC

Accommodation

PARK PLAZA HOTEL
4 Avenue Rd
Toronto M5R 2E8
Tel. (416) 924 5471
AC, TV, U, R, B, CC

SILVER MOON MOTEL
2157 Lake Shore Blvd W
Toronto M8V 1A1
Tel. (416) 252 5051
AC, TV, CC

TORONTO AIRPORT INTERNATIONAL
5875 Airport Rd
Mississauga L4V 1N1
Tel. (416) 677 9900
AC, G, ISP, OSP, SA, RB, CC, TV, U

NORTH AMERICAN MOTEL
2147 Lake Shore Blvd W
Toronto M8V 1A1
Tel. (416) 255 1127
AC, G, TV, CC

TORONTO INTERNATIONAL HOSTEL
223 Church Street
Toronto M5B 1Z1
Tel. (416) 368 1848
AC, CC

WEST POINT MOTOR HOTEL
2285 Lake Shore Blvd W
Toronto M8V 1A6
Tel. (416) 259 1138
AC, OSP, TV, U, B, R, CC

Quetico Prov. Park

NIAGARA FALLS

ALPINE MOTEL
7742 Lundys Lane
Niagara L2H 1H1
Tel. (416) 356 7016
AC, G, ISP, TV, CC

AMBASSADOR MOTEL
6471 Stanley Avenue S
Niagara L2G 3Y6
Tel. (416) 635 0651
AC, G, ISP, TV, CC

AMERI-CANA MOTOR INN
8444 Lundys Lane
Niagara L2H 1H4
Tel. (416) 356 8444
AC, G, OSP, T, TV, R,
B, CC

ASTON VILLA MOTEL
7939 Lundys Lane
Niagara L2H 1H3
Tel. (416) 357 3535
AC, G, OSP, TV, CC

BEST WESTERN
CAIRN CROFT HOTEL
6400 Lundys Lane
Niagara L2G 1T6
Tel. (416) 356 1161
AC, G, ISP, TV, U, R,
B, CC

BEST WESTERN
YOUR HOST MOTOR HOTEL
5551 Murray Street
Niagara L2G 2J4
Tel. (416) 356 0551
AC, G, ISP, OSP, SA, R,
B, TV, U, WP, CC

BLACKSTONE INN MOTEL
5643 Ellen Avenue
Niagara L2G 3P5
Tel. (416) 357 3681
AC, G, OSP, SA, TV,
WP, CC

THE BROCK HOTEL
AT MAPLE LEAF RESORT
5685 Falls Avenue
Niagara L2E 6W7
Tel. (416) 374 4444
AC, G, TV, U, R, B, CC

BUDGET MOTOR INN
5410 Buchanan Ave
Niagara L2E 5A9
Tel. (416) 354 5814
AC, G, SA, TV, R, B, CC

CAMELOT INN
5640 Stanley Avenue
Niagara L2G 3X5
Tel. (416) 354 3754
AC, G, OSP, TV, CC

CANUCK MOTOR INN
5334 Kitchener Avenue
Niagara L2G 1B5
Tel. (416) 358 8221
AC, G, OSP, R, B, SA,
TV, CC

CARRIAGE HOUSE
MOTOR LODGE
8004 Lundys Lane
Niagara L2H 1H1
Tel. (416) 356 7799
AC, G, ISP, OSP, SA, TV,
U, WP, CC

CATARACT MOTEL
6276 Main Street
Niagara L2G 6A4
Tel. (416) 358 8132
AC, G, OSP, TV, WP, CC

ECONO LODGE
BY THE FALLS
5781 Victoria Avenue
Niagara L2G 3L6
Tel. (416) 356 2034
AC, G, ISP, TV, WP, R,
B, CC

EMPRESS MOTEL & RESTAURANT
5951 Clark Street
Niagara L2G 3W4
Tel. (416) 356 4860
AC, G, ISP, SA, R, B, TV, WP, CC

HOWARD JOHNSON VICTORIA PLACE
5905 Victoira Avenue
Niagara L2G 2L5
Tel. (416) 357 4040
AC, G, ISP, OSP, SA, TV, U, WP, R, B, CC

MELODY MOTEL
13065 Lundys Lane
Niagara L2E 6S4
Tel. (416) 227 1023
AC, G, OSP, TV, CC

THE OLD STONE INN
5425 Robinson Street
Niagara L2G 7L6
Tel. (416) 357 1234
AC, G, OSP, TV, U, CC, R, B

PARK HOTEL
4960 Clifton Hill
Niagara L2G 3P1
Tel. (416)358 3293
AC, G, ISP, OSP, TV, R, B, U, WP, CC

QUALITY INN FALLSWAY
4946 Clifton Hill
Niagara L2E 6S8
Tel. (416) 358 3601
AC, G, ISP, OSP, TV, R, B, WP, CC

BONANZA MOTEL LTD
6267 Lundys Lane
Niagara L2G 1T5
Tel. (416) 356 5135
AC, G, TV, OSP, CC

SPACE MOTEL
8618 Lundys Lane
Niagara L2H 1H4
Tel. (416) 356 3216
AC, G, OSP, TV, CC

CONTINENTAL INN
5756 Ferry Street
Niagara L2G 1S7
Tel. (416) 356 2449
AC, G, OSP, TV, CC

SURFSIDE INN
3665 Macklem Street
Niagara L2G 6C8
Tel. (416) 295 4354
AC, TV, CC

DIPLOMAT MOTOR INN
5983 Stanley Avenue
Niagara L2T 3Y2
Tel. (416)357 9564
AC, G, OSP, TV, CC

VOYAGEUR INN MOTEL
7074 Lundys Lane
Niagara L2G 1W2
Tel. (416) 356 6565
AC, G, TV, CC

Kensington Market

PART IV
Practical Information

PRACTICAL INFORMATION

A-Z Summary

ADVANCE PLANNING 117
    Documents 117
    Employment or Study 118
    Clothing 118
    Odds and Ends 119
    Medical Tips 119
    Drugs 119
    Vaccination 119
BOOKSHOPS 144
CRIME 141
CURRENCY 121
CUSTOMS 120
    Duty Free Imports 120
ELECTRICITY 124
ENTERTAINMENT 124
    Art Galleries and Museums 124
    Children's Entertainment 129
    Cinemas 129
    Theatre and Auditoria 129
    Theatre and Dinning 130
ENTRY REGULATIONS 120
EXHIBITIONS 131
FESTIVALS, GLOBAL FUN 132
    Public Holidays 134
GETTING AROUND TORONTO 135
GETTING AROUND OUTSIDE TORONTO 136
GETTING TO CANADA 122
HELP 138
    Consulates 138
    Medical Emergencies 140
    Police Emergencies 140
    Death 140
    Lost Property 140
    Replacement of Items 140
    Traveller's Cheques 141
LIBRARIES 141
METRIC SYSTEM, THE 176
MOTORING 142
PHOTOGRAPHY 162
POST OFFICE 144
RADIO/TELEVISION 134
RELIGIOUS SERVICES 145
RESTAURANTS AND NIGHTLIFE 148

Toronto Nightlife 157
Niagara Nightlife 162
SEMINARS 134
SHOPPING 163
Markets 164
Antiquites 166
SPORTS AND ATHLETICS 166
TELEPHONE AND TELEGRAPH 168
TIME 169
TIPPING 170
TOURIST SERVICES 170
TOURS 172

View of Toronto from the Islands

Advance Planning

The **Canadian Consulate-General** in your home country, **Canadian Airlines International** and your travel agent will assist you in planning your visit to Toronto and other parts of Canada.

What to bring

Documents

Visitors, with the exception of United States citizens, permanent residents of the USA, who enter Canada from St. Pierre and Miquelon, citizens of France living in and entering from these places, and residents of Greenland entering from there, must have a valid passport. Some people need a Canadian visa and applications and valid documents can be arranged by the Canadian High Commission, Embassy or Consulate in their own country.

The following foreign nationals do NOT require a visa to enter Canada. These are people from Andorra, Antigua and Barbuda, Argentina, Australia, Austria, Bahamas, Belgium, Belize, Bolivia, Botswana, Brazil, Costa Rica, Cyprus, Denmark, Dominican Republic, Fiji, Finland, France, Gambia, Federal Republic of Germany, Greece, Grenada, Honduras, Iceland, Ireland, Israel, Italy, Japan, Kenya, Kiribati, Lesotho, Liechtenstein, Luxembourg, Malawi, Malaysia, Malta, Mauritius, Mexico, Monaco, Nauru, The Netherlands, New Zealand, Nicaragua, Norway, Panama, Papua-New Guinea, Paraguay, Portugal, San Marino, Saudi Arabia, Seychelles Republic, Sierra Leone, Singapore, Solomon Islands, Spain, St. Kitts and Nevis, St. Lucia, St. Vincent, Surinam, Swaziland, Sweden, Switzerland, Tanzania, Tonga, Trinidad and Tobago, Turkey, Tuvalu, United States, Uruguay, Vanuatu, Venezuela, Western Samoa, Zambia and Zimbabwe.

The list also includes British citizens and British overseas citizens who are re-admissible to the United Kingdom and citizens of the British dependent territories who gain citizenship through birth, descent, registration or naturalization in Anguilla, Bermuda, British Virgin Islands, Cayman Islands, Falkland Islands, Gibralta, Hong Kong, Montserrat, Pitcairn Island, St. Helena or the Turks and Caicos Islands.

Visitors entering Canada via the United States need a valid passport and some may need a visa issued in their home country before arrival in the United States.

> **INFOTIP:** If you plan to visit the United States, do not think that you can change your travel plans and automatically enter Canada after your American experience.

Documents will only be issued in an emergency by Canadian consulates in the U.S. at Atlanta, Boston, Buffalo, Chicago, Cleveland, Dallas, Detroit, Los Angeles, Minneapolis, New Orleans, New York City, Philadelphia, San Francisco and Seattle, or by the Canadian Embassy in Washington, D.C. There can even be more complications. If you appear that you do not have sufficient funds to support yourself in Canada, you may be denied entry from the United States by a Canadian immigration official at a border crossing.

Normal visa requirements enable the visitor to stay in Canada for three months.

Employment or study

It can take up to six months through the Canadian High Commission, Embassy or Consulate in your home country to gain authorization to work or study in Canada. A work permit will be valid only if supported by one employer for one job. If you are at all confused, contact the Canadian authority in your own country, or write to Canada Immigration Division, Canada Employment and Immigration Commission, Ottawa, Ontario, Canada, K1A OJ9.

Also bring credit cards.

Americans may need receipts of purchases in Canada for their own customs. All foreigners should check with their own customs departments on current legislation on the importation of certain Canadian purchases such as animal furs, etc.

Clothing

Canada's climatic conditions vary greatly because of the country's huge area. In summer, most hotels, restaurants, shops and public buildings are air conditioned while they are heated in winter along with railway stations, airports and bus terminals. Toronto can be steamy in summer and snow-covered in winter. While days can be warm in other parts of Ontario, bring medium to heavyweight garments, particularly if camping or enjoying outdoor adventure sports.

Basically, be guided by the following. May has warm days, but it can be cool at night. June, July and August are the warmest months. September days can be sunny but the nights can be cool. From October to April, winter apparel applies both day and night.

Odds and Ends

A towel for swimming. Top hotels with pools provide them to guests (some free, others for a small fee) but more modest establishments do not. Pack a portable clothes line, health (see below) and personal necessities such as spectacles, contact lenses and sun cream. If spending time outdoors in summer, bring insect repellent. Do not underestimate the cold of a Canadian winter. Visitors not accustomed to snow and ice should not forget gloves, scarf, warm hat and topcoat or parka. Also pack sensible walking shoes, no matter the season.

Medical Tips

Take out adequate health cover in your travel insurance. Should you become ill, you will need it against private hospital care or the attentions of a hotel's doctor whose charges may be high. Naturally, keep all receipts for fees charged to present on your return. Canada's medical and hospital services are excellent but hospitalization can be VERY expensive with some hospitals adding surcharges for foreign patients.

Take note of the generic names of any prescription drugs to show to a pharmacist in case you run out or lose them.

Ask your doctor to prescribe medications against most unfortunate contigencies. Your kit should include preparations for diarrhoea, constipation, nausea and vomiting and a broad spectrum antibiotic against the type of infections you could pick up at home. Include analgesics.

> **INFOTIP:** If you are subject to spring and early summer hay fever, bring the medication that suits you best. Some areas of southern Ontario can precipitate attacks.

Drugs

Do not bring narcotic drugs to Canada. Penalties are severe.

Vaccinations

No vaccinations are necessary before entering Canada unless one has been in a smallpox affected area within two weeks of the date of arrival in Canada.

Old Fort York

Entry Regulations

See also above under Documents.

Customs

Duty Free Imports

Visitors to Canada over 19 years of age may import
1.1 litre (40 ounzes) of liquor or wine
or 8.2 litres (288 ounzes) of beer.
Visitors 16 years or more can bring 200 cigarettes,
50 cigars and 1 kilo (2.2 pounds) of tobacco.
Over 16, one can import a hunting rifle or shotgun and 200
rounds of ammunition for legitimate recreational use.

You will need a permit to use the weapon and it should be
documented to save hassles when returning to your own
country.

Fully automatic weapons and guns less than 66 cm (26 inches) in barrel length are prohibited.

Personal baggage may include fishing, camping, boating and snow sports and other sports equipment.

Also a radio, television set, musical instrument, typewriter and cameras for personal use during your visit are allowed entry duty free.

Gifts for friends and relatives living in Canada can be imported by visitors free of duty and tax, provided the value of each gift does not exceed $C40, and that the gift is not alcohol, tobacco or advertizing material. Gifts of greater value will be subjected to regular duty and taxes on the excess.

Pets: If you bring a dog or cat over three months of age to Canada via the United States, it must be accompanied by a rabies vaccination certificate signed within the past year by a qualified veterinary surgeon.

International visitors may not import plants or plant materials without a Plant Quarantine Act authorization.

Animal, plant, vegetable, fruit and meat and their products must be declared to customs at the first Canadian entry point.

Currency

There is no limit on the amount of foreign currency that can be taken to Canada.

Canadian currency is based on the decimal system. Notes are issued in $1, $2, $5, $20, $50, $100, $500 and $1000 denominations. Coins are 1 cent, 5 cents (nickel) 10 cents (dime) 25 cents (quarter) 50 cents and the rarely encountered silver dollar.

> **INFOTIP:** If you are buying travellers' cheques outside of Canada, try to gain them in Canadian dollars because Canadian banks levy a significant charge for cashing travellers' cheques in any other currency but their own.

Visitors can change money at banks, trust companies, credit unions or exchange booths at airports and border crossing points. Banks offer the best rate of exchange. It is best to shop and pay for services with Canadian currency or credit card as some restaurants and shops will not accept travellers' cheques. You may have to pay for the phone call to determine the current exchange rate.

Harbour Front

Getting To Canada

By Air

Canada is connected by air from all parts of the world. Flights may be through or via transfers from connecting airports. There are also some air charters. mainly from Europe and the USA. Canada's internationally-connected airports are at Toronto, Calgary, Edmonton, Gander, Halifax, Montreal, Ottawa, Regina, Vancouver and Winnipeg. These have excellent facilities and are mostly served by airport hotels.

If you are arriving in Toronto by air from Peterborough, Hamilton, Montreal or Ottawa, you may land at Toronto Island Airport, particularly if you are coming by private aircraft. Landing fees and customs information can be gained by
Tel.(416) 868-6942. For City Express Air Services to and from the centres above, Tel. 977-0000.

From this airport, you will arrive in Toronto by special ferry at the foot of Bathurst Street.

By Rail

You can reach Toronto by train from Vancouver on the Canadian Pacific coast and from other provinces. You can enter also from the USA. There is a rail link from the USA to Canada via Amtrak and other American railway lines at border crossings. VIA Rail provides services throughout Canada and all tracks leading to Toronto converge at Union Station at Front and Bay Streets. Tel. 366-8411. Go Transit (Tel: 630-3933) has regular GO bus and train services from (and to) Ontario's Oshoawa, Hamilton, Georgetown, Brampton. Milton, Newmarket and Richmond Hill and limited services from and to Barrie Guelph, Sutton and Uxbridge.

By Road

You can arrive from the USA border by bus and private or rental car. In Toronto, intercity buses arrive at and depart from the Bus Terminal, 610, Bay Street. Tel: Gray Coach Lines, 979-3511.

There are so many crossing points from the USA that it is impractical to list them in this guide. If arriving from the US in a rental car and/or trailer (caravan) or mobile home, you will need to bring with your vehicle registration forms and a copy of the rental contract to show that vehicle use in Canada is authorized by the rental company. Should you be in a vehicle lent to you by an American friend, you must carry a letter from the owner authorizing you to use his/her vehicle in Canada.

A security deposit may be necessary at the border to ensure you return the vehicle to the USA. An alternative is for visitors to gain a carnet de passage en duane (a ticket of customs passage) issued in your home country.

The under-side of any vehicles imported from other countries will need to be steam-cleaned on arrival to remove any adhering soil. Vehicle shippers will advize where this can be done and issue a steam-cleaning certificate.

> **INFOTIP:** If you rent or borrow a car in the USA to take to Canada, ensure that it does not have studded tyres. These are detrimental to Canada's excellent and well-maintained highways and are prohibited.

By Sea

While passenger liners are infrequent arrivals at Canadian ports, it is still possible to reach Canada by sea across the Pacific and Atlantic Oceans on a luxury liner or passenger-carrying freighter. You should inquire about this possibility from a travel agent in your home country.

Marineland, Nigara Falls

Electricity

The elctric current in Canada is 110 volts and 60 Hz. It is AC almost everywhere.

> **INFOTIP:** Transformers are widely available in Canadian electrical supply stores for the use of foreign electrical appliances.

Entertainment

Art Galleries and Museums

Toronto has major museums and such a proliferation of art galleries, large and small, that making choices can be bewildering. For greater detail on the most prominent of these, see also the Touring section of this InfoGuide. The following list of musea also includes historical homes and sites.

Campbell House, 160, Queen St West. Tel: 597-0227. Open weekends and holidays noon to 4.30 p.m. Weekdays 9.30 a.m. to 11.30 a.m. and 2.30 p.m. to 4.30 p.m. Admission is charged.

Casa Loma, 1, Austin Terrace Tel: 923-1171.
Open 10 a.m. to 4 p.m. daily. Admission is charged.

Colborne Lodge, High Park (South side) Tel: 392-6916.
Open Monday to Saturday 9.30 a.m. to 5 p.m. Sunday and
holidays noon to 5 p.m. Admission free.

Enoch Turner School House, 106 Trinity St. Tel: 863-0010.
Toronto's first free school, built in 1848, is a cultural and
social centre. Open weekdays from 10 a.m. to 4 p.m.
Small admission charge.

Fort York, Garrison Ave. Tel: 392-6907.
Open Monday to Saturday 9.30 a.m. to 5 p.m.
Sundays and holidays noon to 5 p.m.
Admission charged.

Gibson House, 5172, Yonge St. Tel: 225-0146.
Open weekdays 9.30 a.m. to 5 p.m.
Weekends and holidays noon to 5 p.m.
Admission charged.

The Grange, 317, Dundas St. West.
Tel: 977-0414, ext 237.
Open Tuesday to Sunday 11 a.m. to 5.30 p.m. and to 9 p.m.
on Sunday.
Admission gives entrance to the Art Gallery of Ontario.
Free on Wednesdays.

Practical Information

Mackenzie House, 82, Bond St. Tel: 392-6915.
Open Monday to Saturday 9.30 a.m. to 5 p.m.
Sunday noon to 5 p.m. Admission charged.

Montgomery's Inn, 4709, Dundas St. West.
Tel: 394-8113. Restored Georgian inn circa 1847.
Open weekdays 9.30 a.m. to 4.30 p.m.
Weekends 1 p.m. to 5 p.m. Admission charged.

Spadina Estate, 285, Spadina Rd. Tel: 392-6910.
Open Monday to Saturday 9.30 a.m. to 5 p.m.
Sunday and holidays noon to 5 p.m. Admission charged.

Todmorden Mills Museum, 67, Pottery Rd. Tel: 425-2250.
Open 11 a.m. to 5 p.m. weekends. Closed Monday.
Tuesday to Friday 10 a.m. to 5 p.m. Admission charged.

Toronto's First Post Office, 260, Adelaide St. East.
Tel: 865-1822. Open daily from 10 a.m. to 4 p.m. Free.

Canada Sports Hall of Fame, Centre of Exhibition Place.
Tel: 595-1046. Open Tuesday to Sunday 10 a.m. to 4.30
p.m. Closed Monday. Free.

Canadian Decorative Arts, Sigmund Samuel Building,
14, Queen's Park Crescent West. Tel: 586-5549.
Open Monday to Saturday 10 a.m. to 5 p.m.
Sunday 1 p.m. to 5 p.m. Free.

George R. Gardiner Museum of Ceramic Art, 111,
Queen's Park.
Tel: 593-9300. Open Tuesday to Sunday 10 a.m. to 5 p.m.
Admission (which includes entrance to the main building
of the Royal Ontario Museum.)

George Scott Railton Heritage Centre, The Salvation Army,
2130, Bayview Ave. Tel: 481-4441.
Artifacts and documents on the Salvation Army's work in
Canada and Bermuda. Open Monday to Friday 8.30 a.m.
to 4.30 p.m. Otherwise by appointment. Free.

Hockey Hall of Fame and Museum, Exhibition Place.
Tel: 595-1345.
Open Tuesday to Sunday 10 a.m to 4.30 p.m. Closed
Monday. Admission charged.

Marine Museum of Upper Canada, Exhibition Place.
Tel: 392-6827.
Open Monday to Saturday 9.30 a.m. to 5 p.m.
Sunday and holidays noon to 5 p.m. Admission charged.

Market Gallery, South St. Lawrence Market, 95, Front St. East.
Tel: 392-7604.
Open Wednesday to Friday 10 a.m. to 4 p.m.
Saturday 9 a.m. to 4 p.m. Sunday noon to 4 p.m.
Closed Monday, Tuesday and holidays. Free.

Museum of the History of Medicine, 288, Bloor St. West.
Tel: 922-0564. Open Monday to Friday 9.30 a.m. to 4.p.m.
Free.

Redpath Sugar Museum, 95, Queen's Quay East.
Tel: 366-3561 extension 323.
Open Monday to Friday 10 a.m. to noon and 1 p.m. to 3.30 p.m. Free.

Royal Ontario Museum (ROM) 100, Queen's Park.
Tel: 586-5549.
Open daily 10 a.m. to 6 p.m. with the exception of Tuesday and Thursday when it remains open until 8 p.m.
Admission charged but this includes entrance to the George R. Gardiner Museum of Ceramic Art.

William Ashley Crystal Museum, 50, Bloor St. West.
Tel: 964-2900.
Selected and commissioned works exhibiting the art of glass by international artisans.
Open Monday to Wednesday 10 a.m. to 6 p.m. Thursday and Friday 10 a.m. to 7.30 p.m. Saturday 9.30 a.m. to 5.30 p.m. Closed Sunday. Free.

Ontario Science Centre, 770, Don Mills Rd. Tel: 429-4100.
Open daily from 10 a.m. to 6 p.m.
Remains open on Friday to 9p.m.
Admission charged, but free from 6 p.m. to 9 p.m. on Friday.

Art Gallery of Ontario, 317, Dundas St. West.
Tel: 977-0414.
Open Tuesday to Sunday 11 a.m. to 5.30 p.m.
Remains open until 9 p.m. Wednesday. Closed Monday.
Admission charged every day except Wednesday.

Del Bello Gallery, 363, Queen St. West. Tel: 593-0884.
Contemporary Canadian sculptures, paintings and original hand-printed, limited editions. Open daily. Free.
The Inuit Gallery of Eskimo Art, 9, Prince Arthur Ave.
Tel: 921-9985. Open Monday to Saturday 10 a.m. to 6 p.m.
Free.

Practical Information

The Isaacs Gallery, 179, John St. (First floor)
Tel: 595-0770.
Early North American Indian art and contemporary Canadian.
Open 10 a.m. to 6 p.m. Tuesday to Saturday.

Joseph D. Carrier Art Gallery, Columbus Centre, 901, Lawrence Ave. West. Tel: 789-7011.
Works from antique to modern by national and international artists in a unique, rotunda gallery. Open daily.

Julianne Galleries of Fine Art, Scarborough Town Centre. Tel: 296-5410. Eskimo sculpture and Canadian arts and crafts. Open Monday to Friday 9.30 a.m. to 9.30 p.m. Saturday 9.30 a.m. to 6 p.m. Free.

Toronto Sculpture Garden, 115, King St. East.
Tel: 485-9658.
Outdoor contemporary sculptures. Open daily 8 a.m. to dusk. Free.

The Craft Gallery (Ontario Crafts Council) 346, Dundas St. West. Tel: 977-3551. Monthly exhibits of traditional or contemporary ceramics, glass, fibre, wood, leather and metal crafts. Open Tuesday to Saturday 10 a.m. to 5 p.m.
Sunday 2 p.m. to 5 p.m. Closed Monday. Free.

Niagara-On-The-Lake

Children's Entertainment

See Touring section for details on Centreville, Black Creek Pioneer Village, Toronto Zoo, Harbourfront, Exhibition Place, Fort York, Ontario Place, McLaughlin Planetarium, Sunshine Beach Water Park, Canada's Wonderland, Ontario Science Centre, Maritime Museum, CN Tower, Canada's and the Hockey Halls of Fame and High Park. Also the Toronto Public Library Boys and Girls' House at 40, St. George St. has the Osborne Collection of early children's books from the 14th century. Tel: 593-5350. Open Monday to Friday 10 a.m. to 6 p.m. Saturday 9 a.m. to 5 p.m. Closed Sunday. Free.

There is very little in Toronto that junior visitors will not enjoy with their parents. Kids will go ape at everything in Niagara Falls. The trick will be to restrict the number of entertainments.

Babysitting: Inquire from Housekeeping at your hotel.

INFOTIP: For current news on absolutely everything that is happening in Toronto during your visit, telephone 1212 and you will be told the headlines of the day, all the entertainment available, including sporting events and, heaven forbid, a directory of the soap operas on TV!

Cinemas

The downtown area of Toronto and the cities and borough of Metro Toronto have scores of cinemas. Rather than list them all, we suggest you consult the entertainment pages of the daily newspapers for the movie and location of your choice. All newspaper advertisements give addresses and telephone numbers.

Canada produces some excellent films in English and French so it would be good to see at least one, just in case it takes an age to reach your home country. Movies fresh from the USA and the rest of the world in their languages, with sub-titles, are also screened.

Theatres and Auditoria

O'Keefe Centre, 1. Front St. East. Tel: 393-7469.
Toronto's largest theatre. Broadway musics, comedies, revues, the Canadian Opera Company and the National Ballet.

Royal Alexandra Theatre, 260, King St. West.
Tel: 593-4211. From Shakespeare to musicals.

Practical Information

Massey Hall, 178, Victoria St. Tel: 363-7301.
Concert performances and other shows.

Roy Thomson Hall, 60, Simcoe St. Tel: 977-7107.
Home of the Toronto Symphony Orchestra and performances including comedy and pop concerts.

Toronto Truck Theatre Productions, 94, Belmont St.
Tel: 922-0084. A Toronto institution for drama.

Toronto Free Theatre, 26, Berkeley St. Tel: 368-2856.
Contemporary and class theatre.

St.Lawrence Centre for the Arts, 26, Front St. East.
Tel: 366-7723. Two theatres for music, dance, plays, public forums and films. Also Theatre Plus has summer season contemporary plays at 49, Front St. Tel: 869-1255.

Bayview Playhouse, 1605, Bayview Ave., East York.
Tel: 481-6191. Year-round comedies and musicals.

Factory Theatre, 125, Bathurst St. Tel: 864-9971.
Contemporary Canadian productions.

Leah Posulns Theatre, 4588, Bathurst St, North York.
Tel: 630-6752. Musicals and drama.

INFOTIP: For current up-dates on theatre and music in Toronto, check the daily newspapers and also the Metropolitan Toronto annual Visitors' Guide and Events Guide published four times annually.

Also the regular Dining and Nightlife Guide. These are published by the Metropolitan Convention and Visitors' Association, 220, Yonge St. Tel: 979-3133. The monthly commercial magazines Toronto and Toronto Life have comprehensive entertainment listings and advertizements. As well, Now, a newspaper on Toronto's weekly news and entartainments, is distributed free.

Theatre Dining

Another first for Toronto is that it is the Comedy Capital of North America. Theatre dining in the city includes three establishments where you may laugh until you cry and maybe even choke on your dinner - but not because it isn't any good! The funniest place in town is: Second City, 110 Lombard St. Tel: 863-1111.
Performances have received rave reviews since this 'Temple of Satire' opened in 1973.

Botanical Gardens, Hamilton

Another venue is Harper's Dinner Theatre at 38, Lombard St. Tel: 863-6223.

Also, Yuk Yuk's Comedy Kabaret, 1280, Bay St., Yorkville. Tel: 967-6425.
   More dinner theatres are listed under Restaurants and Nightlife.

Exhibitions

   Toronto is a major North American venue for many and varied regular and one-off exhibitions. For details of what is on display, where and when, coinciding with your visit to the city, telephone for current information to Metropolitan Toronto Convention and Visitors' Association, Queen's Quay at Harbourfront, Tel.368-9990.
   However, regular, important exhibitions include:
   Metro International Caravan, displaying the traditions of more than 50 international cultures at pavilions throughout the city. It is held in the last two weeks of June. Tel: 977-0466.

Canadian National Exhibition, the oldest and largest annual exhibition in the world, featuring agricultural and technical exhibits and entertainments held in the historical Exhibition Building, Exhibition Place, Lakeside Boulevard West, from mid-August to early September.

Royal Agricultural Winter Fair. This is North America's outstanding agricultural exhibition, including the Royal Horse Show. At Colosseum, Exhibition Place, the 10-day event takes place in mid-November.
See also BUSINESS GUIDE. For cultural exhibitions, see Art Galleries and Museums.

FESTIVALS, GLOBAL FUN

One could call the multi-cultural Metro International Caravan featuring arts, crafts, exotic foods and drink, theatre, jazz, choirs and dance a festival. See above.
Caribana: Toronto's giant annual West Indian festival. This is held yearly in the week leading up to the August Civic Holiday. The opening parade creates a frenzy down the length of University Avenue on its way to the Toronto Islands and principally Centre Island which is the festival's main location. Entertainments include music, spectacular dance, impromptu performances by Torontonians and floating nightclubs cruising Lake Ontario.

> **INFOTIP:** Ticketed events sell out quickly, so reserve them at the Caribana office, Suite 213, 2, Gloucester St. Tel: 925-5435.

Mariposa: This is a series of year-round events planned by the Mariposa Folk Foundation which operates a Toronto concert season as well as occasional festivals and events. These include concerts for children and free summer performances in the parks. Events include traditional music, dance, story-telling, theatre, craft exhibitions and children's performances highlighting international origins. For events, venues and times,
Tel.363-4009.

International Picnic: Annually from late June to early July, Exhibition Place is the venue for one huge, family day. You must pack your own picnic but there is no admission charge. Entertainment includes pizza and yoghurt-eating contests, music, dance, soccer games, wrestling bouts, a Miss Bikini Pageant and the chance to meet Torontonians in festival mood.

The Annual Film Festival: This is usually scheduled for September. It lasts about 10 days and includes all manner of movies, special events and appearances by popular movie stars. Gain more information from the newspapers and the Metropolitan Toronto Convention and Visitors' Association.

The Annual Molson Jazz Festival: In late July or early August, this festival fills Harbourfront with three days and nights of music. It is free.

See also the Sidetrip Tour section of this InfoGuide. For details of the Shaw Festival from April to October at Niagara-On-The-Lake, telephone in Toronto Tel.790-7301.

There is also the Stratford Festival from May to October at the town of Stratford about one hour's drive from Toronto. For information, write to Box 520, Stratford, 0N N5A 6V2 or
Tel. (519) 271-4040 or, in Toronto, 364-8355.
Niagara Falls' Winter Festival of Light runs from late November to late February.

Public Holidays

These holidays are common throughout Canada. They are:-

New Year's Day,
Good Friday,
Easter Monday,
Victoria Day (mid-May)
Canada Day (July 1)
Labour Day (early September)
Thanksgiving (mid-October)
Remembrance Day (November 11)
Christmas Day and Boxing Day.

Ontario also has a Civic Holiday in the first week of August.

Radio/Television

Toronto is blessed with so many television and radio stations, some of them operating 24 hours a day, that all you have to do is twiddle the dial.

Daily newspapers publish programme details and the better hotels provide this service information in their rooms.

Seminars

Details of seminars and workshops will be found in Toronto's daily newspapers. Check for details.

Getting Around Toronto

It is easy and there are several alternatives to get around this huge city. The Toronto Transit Subway System or TTC has a good network which emanates from the heart of the downtown area to the main suburbs. The subway is also incorporated with buses or streetcars (trams) which will take you to areas where the subway will not.

INFOTIP: Gain your transfer from subway to bus or streetcar when you pay your first fare. Transfer should be with the hour of commencing the journey but one ticket should take you wherever the combined system reaches.

If beginning the trip with bus or streetcar, you will need to give the exact fare as drivers do not carry change. Best is to gain tickets and/or tokens at subway stations.

There are 63 stations in the Toronto subway system running approximately north-south and east-west.

You can obtain information on how to reach any point on this transit system by calling TTC Information on 393-INFO between 7 a.m. and 11.30 p.m., daily, year-round.

GO (Government of Ontario) Transit Trains go beyond the limits of the city as far west as Hamilton, north to Richmond Hill and Georgetown and east to Pickering. A GO bus has an extension service from these cities and towns and the system connects with TTC's subway system at Union Station on Front Street.

If you need to get to Toronto's Lester B. Pearson International Airport by bus, buses leave from Islington, York Mills and Yorkdale subway stations. A regular bus service will also pick up about every 20 minutes from certain downtown hotels for the airport. Naturally, the service operates in reverse.

For information on buses from the subways and hotels, Tel. 979-3511. *You can travel from the easterly terminal of the Bloor-Danforth subway line at Kennedy Road and Eglinton Avenue for 7 km to the Scarborough City Centre by Scarborough's Rapid Transit. For information, contact MTCVA.* Tel: 979-3143.

Ferries

For the Toronto Islands, ferries leave from Bay Street behind the Harbour Castle Westin Hotel. Tel: 392-8193 for schedules. From Harbourfront to Ontario Place, there is a water shuttle operated by Gray Line Harbour and Island Tours. Shuttles leave and return hourly. Tel: 364-2412.

Taxis

Because Toronto has not allowed any recent development of freeways, road traffic tends to be comgested and slow moving at peak times and during the day, one reason you should discount renting a car if you are staying in the downtown area. Taxis, while not the most efficient way of getting around, are really handy at night to take you to the various, far-flung entertainments of the metropolis.

Taxis tend not to cruise the Toronto streets. It is much more satisfactory for you to get your hotel desk or a restaurant owner to call you one.

Well-heeled Canadians are also into using limousines and there is nothing nicer than sitting back in the rear of a stretched limo, sipping champagne to prepare you for an evening flight out of Pearson Airport.

Some taxi companies are Co-op Cabs. Tel: 364-81561.

Another group of companies, Metro Cab has 800 cars and 24-hour service. Tel: 363-5757.

A third is Diamond Taxi Cab Association. Tel: 366-6868.

Limousines

House of Limousines Inc., 145. Front St. East. Tel: 364-6199.

Also Reliable Limousine and Executive Services Ltd., 73, Grange Ave. Tel: 977-4811.

Getting Around Outside Toronto

By Air

You can leave Toronto via the City Express to Peterborough, Hamilton, Montreal and Ottawa from Toronto Island airport. For information, Tel.977 0000.

Toronto's Pearson Airport is in the north-west corner of Metro Toronto and accessible from Highways 401, 427 and 409. Many major airlines have regular flights in and out of Toronto from here to all parts of Canada and much of the world. (See Part V)

> **INFOTIP:** For the most current information on air traffic, tune your radio to Airport Radio Information Service, CFYZ number 530 on the AM dial.

By Rail

VIA Rail at Union Station provides services throughout Canada. Tel: 366-8411.

GO Transit has regular train services to some places in Ontario. See Getting Around Toronto. Tel: 630-3933.

By Road

Out of town buses depart from the Bus Terminal, 610, Bay St. at Dundas. Inter-city and intra-province bus companies include Gray Coach Line, 154, Front St. East. Tel: 979-3531. Services to all points in Canada or the USA.

By Water

Pleasure craft can enter Canada from the USA by boat-trailer or under their own power. An entry permit will be issued by Canadian Customs. It must be returned on departure. Boats powered by motors 7.5 kw/10 HP or more must be licensed and the number clearly displayed on both sides of the vessel's bow. Boat licences from outside Ontario are acceptable. Overboard discharge of rubbish or untreated sewage is prohibited.

There are several companies which will crew for you on charter. These include Great Lakes Yacht Charters, Berth 7, Pier 6, 145, Queen's Quay West. Tel: 460-6024. Up to 15 people accommodated on a modern cruiser which is available for charter by the hour, day or week.

Help!

Consulates

Consular activities carried on in Toronto are listed below. These services exist by agreement with the Government of Canada and are bound by certain Canadian regulations, as well as by orders from their home countries.

Questions regarding:
Visas and passports.
Citizenship, dual nationality, dual status.
Military service status or dual nationalty persons.
Difficulties with local regulations (Customs, the law etc.)
Assistance with absentee voting in your home country.
Notarization or witnessing of documents.
Assistance in the case of death.
Assistance with repatriation problems.

Consulates should be notified in case of hospitalization of a foreigner if the nationality of the patient is known.

In case of arrest in Canada, your embassy in Ottawa or consulate in Toronto (if there is one) should be notified. Both Canadians and foreign visitors are subject to the same laws in Canada with the exception of diplomatic persons and ignorance of the law is not a grounds for defence.

However, your consulate may inform you of your rights, notify your family, register complaints on your behalf and try to contact one of the Canadian organizations that visit prisons and are concerned with the welfare of prisoners.

Australian Consulate General. Tel: 323-1155.
Belgium Consulate General, Tel: 364-0649.
Brazilian Consulate, Tel: 922-2503.
British Consulate General, Tel: 593-1267.
Danish Consulate General, Tel: 962-5661.
Finland Consulate General, Tel: 964-0066.
French Consulate General, Tel: 925-8041.
Federal Republic of Germany Consulate General, Tel: 925-2813.
Greek Consulate General, Tel.593-1636.
Indian Consulate General, Tel: 960-0751.
Indonesian Consulate, Tel: 591-6461.
Israel Consulate General, Tel: 961-1126.
Italian Consulate General, Tel: 977-1566.
Japanese Consulate General. Tel: 363-7038.
Malaysian Consulate, Tel: 869-3886.
Maltese Consulate General, Tel: 767-4902.

Niagara-on-the-Lake

Netherlands Consulate General, Tel: 598-2590.
Phillipines Consulate General, Tel: 922-7181.
Portugese Consulate General, Tel: 360-8260.
Republic of South Africa Consulate, Tel: 364-0314.
Spanish Consulate General, Tel: 967-4949.
Switzerland Consulate General, Tel: 593-5371.
Thailand Consulate Genertal, Tel: 367-6750.
United States of America Government Office,
Tel: 595-1700.

Medical Emergencies

Telephone **911**, which is the emergency number for **ambulance, fire** and **police**. Alternatively, call for an **ambulance** on 489-2111.

If you must be admitted to hospital, your consulate will advize on how to handle payment.

> **INFOTIP:** If you have neglected to take out medical insurance before arrival in Toronto, telephone Hospital Medical Care on 597-0666 or Ontario Blue Cross. Tel: 429-2661. These organizations can also give you up-to-date information on which services are provided by Toronto's various hospitals and medical service centres - and what you can expect to pay.

For information relating to the **disabled** call the Community Information Centre. tel: 863-0505.

Should you require non-prescription medications, ask your hotel reception desk for the location of the closest pharmacy (drugstore) Some big hotels have their own.

People who are members of **Medic-Alert** will find assistance at 293, Eglinton St. East. Tel: 481-5175.

Police Emergencies

Tel. 911, or 0, or 324 2222.

Death

A foreign visitor's death in Canada immediate notification to the deceased person's consulate, embassy or high commission by relatives, friends, hotel staff, hospital or police authorities.

Lost Property

Should you lose something in your hotel, report it immediately to the hospitality desk if you are in a large hotel or front desk staff if in a smaller establishment. Otherwise, if you suspect theft, contact the police.

Replacement of Items

If you lose your passport, report it to your consulate immediately.

Credit Cards

Report the loss to the credit card company concerned.

Check with your hotel's front desk for current addresses and telephone numbers in Toronto if you are not a holder of the world's most widely-accepted cards. These are :

Diners Club, Canada Royal Bank, 325, Front St. West. Tel: 974-4447. Lost or stolen cards. Tel: 974-4515.

American Express, 101, McNabb St., Unionville. Tel: 474-8000. Lost or stolen cards. Tel: 474-9280.

Mastercard (Bank of Montreal.) For lost or stolen cards, contact Tel. 232-8020 (24 hours.)

Visa, Canadian Imperial Bank of Commerce, 750, Lawrence Ave. West. Tel: 785-8090.

> **INFOTIP:** As Visa has several outlets in Toronto at different banks, telephone the above number to discover the location most convenient to you.

Travellers' Cheques

Lost or stolen travellers' cheques are usually replaced quickly by the issuing banks or agents. But the swiftness of replacement may depend on what proof you can supply, particularly cheque numbers and receipt for their purchase. Keep these in a separate place in your luggage away from your cheques.

Crime

Toronto is justifiably proud of its low crime, compared with most large North American cities. The rate of violent crime is incredibly low. But should you need the police, just dial O. This applies anywhere in Canada. In addition, in Toronto, you can call 911 or 324-2222 for police assistance.

Libraries

Toronto Public Library, 14, St. George St. Tel: 593-5350. (Also Boys and Girls' House.) Open Monday to Friday 10 a.m. to 6 p.m. Saturday 9 a.m. to 5 p.m.

City of Scarborough Public Library, 1076, Ellesmere St. Tel: 291-1991.

Etobicoke Public Libraries, Islington and Summitcrest. Tel: 248-5681.

North York Public Library, 1520, Yonge St. Tel: 733-5700.

York Public Library, 1745, Eglinton St. West.
Tel: 394-1000.

There are more than 20 other neighbourhood libraries throughout Metro Toronto. Call the Toronto Public Library for advice on the type of books available and the library nearest to you.

Motoring

A valid driver's licence from any country is good in Canada for three months. If you hold membership of the American Automobile Association, you can gain the benefits of any CAA club in Ontario. See Getting Around By Car for more details on motoring in Canada.

INFOTIP: It is not economical to drive a rental car from Toronto to another major city and drop off the vehicle there. You will be involved in steep costs to have the vehicle returned to its Toronto depot.

Canadians drive on the right of the road like Americans below the border. Speed limits in Ontario are 90 to 100 km/h (55-62 mph) in multi-laned, controlled access highways. On two-lane highways, it is 80-90 km/h (50-55 mph.) In urban and populated areas, the speed limit is 40-60 km/h (25-37 mph.) In Ontario, right turns may be made against a red light unless otherwise indicated. You must stop but continue cautiously if the way is clear.

Vehicles travelling in either direction, except for divided highways, must stop for a yellow school bus when its red signal lights are flashing. Also, in Toronto, you must stop at least two metres behind the rear door of a slowing or halted streetcar.

Wearing seatbelts is compulsory. Radar-warning devices are illegal. International bridges, tunnels and ferries connecting with the USA charge fees but Canada's highways, bridges etc. are toll-free.

Should you be involved in an accident, ask someone to call Zenith 50000. If personal injury or property damage is likely to exceed a cost of $C700, you must notify police and remain at the scene of the accident. Information on road conditions are available from the Road Information Office. Tel: 248-3561.

Car Rentals   Rates vary according to the size of the car and whether or not unlimited kilometres are required.

Some firms offer several hundred km free or a daily rate with km charge added. Generally, insurance is extra. Cash deposit or credit card imprint is invariably requested.

If you are travelling out of Toronto's downtown area and particularly taking day excursions for longer trips, renting a car can be an economical and pleasurable way to tour. You will be required to produce your valid driver's licence. Few companies rent vehicles under 21.

INFOTIP: Rush hours in downtown Toronto are 7 a.m. to 9 a.m. and 4 p.m. to 6 p.m. Park only in designated areas as the city has a tow-away policy for parking offenders.

Travelers Rent-A-Car, 241, Church St. Tel: 366-1127. Also Hertz Canada Ltd. Tel: 620-9620.
Budget Car Rentals Toronto Ltd., 5905, Campus Rd., Mississauga. Tel: 676-1240.
To book outside Toronto, toll free 1-800-263-0600.

Owasco Canadian Car & Camper Rental, 1425, Dundas St. East, Whitby. Tel: 668-9383 and in downtown Toronto 683-3235 offers cars, 8 and 12-seater buses, campervans and tent rental with camping equipment. There are free airport and hotel pick-ups and drop-offs.

Bookshops

University of Toronto Bookstore, 214, College St. Tel: 978-7908. This store has 100,000 titles occupying four floors.

World's Biggest Bookstore, 20, Edward St. Tel: 977-7009. With the claim of its name, this store has more than 1 million books on more than 27 km of shelving!

Children's Bookstore, 604, Markham St. Tel: 533-7011. This claims the world's biggest selection of books for children from one month of age (!!) to 17 years.

Broadway and Hollywood Books, 2nd Floor, 17, Yorkville Ave. Tel: 926-8992. Out of print, antiquarian and first edition books available.

Edwards Books and Art, 356, Queen St. West. Tel: 593-0126. Rare, out of print art books and gift books.

There are scores of other bookshops throughout downtown Toronto.

Post Office

Tourism literature, seemingly quaintly, advizes that Canadian stamps must be used to expedite mail within and outside Canada. This, self-evident fact must have been denied by many visitors otherwise authorities would not have bothered to insert it in its literature. So, you are told. Use Canadian stamps.

These stamps can be bought at post offices, hotels, automatic vending machines in some hotel lobbies, railway stations, airports, bus terminals, many stores and some street newspaper stands.

You can find the location of the nearest post office from your hotel reception desk or visit **Toronto's First Post Office**, 260, Adelaide St. East. Or **Canada Post Corporation**, 20, Bay St. Tel: 973-2433. The latter post office is open from 8 a.m. to 6 p.m. and inquiries on post restante facilities should be made here.

> **INFOTIP:** You cannot send telegrammes through post offices in Canada. These (known as Telepost Messages) should be phoned to or delivered to CN/CP Telecommunications. For the nearest office to you, consult your hotel reception desk staff.

Religious Services

As Toronto has more than 500 Christian churches, not to mention Jewish synagogues, Muslim mosques and centres for other major world religions, such as Buddhism, Hinduism and Sikhism, it would be impractical to list them all. If, during your Toronto stay, you wish to attend a religious service, consult church notices in the daily newspapers.

Anglicans and non-Anglicans alike should at least visit **St. Paul's Anglican Church**, 227, Bloor St. East. Tel: 961-8116. Built in early-English gothic style, this historical church, consecrated in 1842, has been enlarged twice. Its cathedral image came after building additions in 1914. It is open daily from noon to 2 p.m.

> **INFOTIP:** For a calming, spiritual interlude, visit at noon on Thursday when St. Paul's presents one-hour pipe organ recitals.

Eaton Centre

Georgian Bay

Restaurants and Nightlife

Representing more than 70 different national groups, Toronto's more than 700 restaurants offer a bewildering array of taste-tempting gastronomic delights. Add to the 70 types of cuisine prepared by residents, who are of foreign birth or descendents of immigrants, Canadian-American style food and other dishes, which hail from the Americas such as Cajun and Californian, and the list of varieties extends.

From a city in which, 40 years ago, it was daring to order meatballs with spaghetti, Toronto has blossomed into a place of pigging-out on a grand international scale. Just imagine. It would take you 35 whole days to sample once the individual cuisines of the 70 different national groups alone, eating both lunch and dinner. We don't include breakfast because it is essentially Canadian-American or English or Continental. So if you are into food, schedule a long stay.

You can eat on the run from one of the many hot-dog or sausage vendors which characterize downtown streets, make up your own picnic from ingredients from one of the city's vital markets, pop in to a bistro or chi-chi Yorkville cafe, be entertained with theatre as you dine or while away an evening above one of the world's most spectacular night panoramas in the highest revolving restaurant on earth.

Before you start eating, here are just a few tips.

If you wish to pay by credit card, check by phone that one of yours is acceptable at the restaurant. Most widely accepted cards are American Express, Diners Club, Mastercard, Visa, Bank Americard, Carte Blanche and Chargex. Most restaurants with credit card facilities indicate them at the entrance.

Most establishments open for lunch between noon and 3 p.m.; a few at 11.30 a.m. Dinner is from 5 p.m. to about 10 p.m. on weekdays but continues as late as 1 a.m. on weekends.

Credit card or Canadian currency is the best method of payment. If the restaurant does change travellers' cheques, the rate will not be ideal.

No one, by law, under the age of 19 will be served alcohol. Drinking hours are from 11 a.m. to 1 a.m. On Sundays, they are from noon to 11 p.m.

Where this InfoGuide advizes if the restaurant is budget-priced, moderate or expensive, this does not take into consideration alcohol. Wine tends to be expensive in Canada. Its own wine industry is fairly small and most establishments rely on imports which are not cheap.

Canada produces some passable beers which are less likely to break the bank.

The following restaurant recommendations are listed alphabetically by national cuisines.

Cajun

Cafe Creole, Skyline Toronto Airport Hotel, 655 Dixon Rd. Tel: 244-1711. Creole and Cajun dishes in the Louisiana traditions. Open daily for breakfast, lunch and dinner from 6.30 a.m. Medium prices.

Zaidy's, 225 Queen St. West. Tel: 977-7222.
Gumbo, crab cakes, shrimp Creole served in the finest Cajun tradition. Open daily for lunch and dinner. Medium to expensive.

Californian

JJ Muggs Gourmet Grille, 1 Dundas St. West.
Tel: 598-4700. Situated in the Eaton Centre, this popular Toronto eatery covers two floors plus an outdoor balcony, serving salads, burgers and sundaes. Open daily for breakfast, lunch and dinner. Inexpensive.

Canadian

Traditions, The Spadina Hotel, 460 King St. West.
Tel: 368-2864. Great Canadian cuisine in a unique dining room circa 1883 that has been restored to its original condition. Open daily for lunch and dinner. Inexpensive to moderate prices.

Chinese

Chinese Palace, 2nd floor, 150 Dundas St. West.
Tel: 977-3751. Cantonese and Szechuan cuisine. Dim sim lunch. Medium price range. Open Monday to Thursday, 11 a.m. to midnight. Friday and Saturday 11 a.m. to 1 a.m. Sunday 11 a.m. to midnight.

Sai Woo Restaurant and Tavern, 130 Dundas St. West.
Tel: 977-4988. One of the city's first Chinese restaurants serving Cantonese dishes at moderate prices. Open daily from 11.30 a.m. to 2.30 a.m.

Young Lok Restaurant, 122 St. Patrick St.
Tel: 593-9819. Traditional Beijing and Szechuan menu, including some Mongolian dishes. Moderate prices. Open daily for lunch and dinner.

Continental

Le Saint Tropez Restaurant, 31 Elm St. Tel: 595-5551.
A Toronto meeting place for expatriate French. Medium
prices. Open Monday to Saturday, 11 a.m. to 1 a.m.

Garbo's Bistro, 1429 Queen St. West. Tel: 593-9870.
Continental cuisine in an Art Nouveau setting. Open daily
from 11.30 a.m. to 1 a.m. Live piano music Friday and
Saturday night and Sunday brunch. Medium prices.

The Old House On Church Street, 582 Church St.
Tel: 925-5316. Fine cuisine in an historical Toronto home.
Average prices. Open daily for lunch and dinner.

Prince Arthur Room, Park Plaza Hotel, 4 Avenue Rd.
Tel: 925-5471. Superb Continental fare with a creative
flare in an elegant setting. Open daily for lunch and dinner.
Above average prices.

Danish

Copenhagen Room, 101 Bloor St. West. Tel: 920-3287.
Traditional and new Danish cuisine. Moderate prices.
Open lunch and dinner Monday to Saturday.

English

Sherlock's Prime Rib Restaurant, 12 Sheppard St.
Tel: 366-8661. Old English decor including stained glass
windows. Specialities include prime rib and Cornish hen.
Open lunch, Monday to Friday. Dinner Monday to
Saturday. Medium prices.

Egyptian

Stone Cottage Inn. 3750 ingston Rd. Tel: 266-6200.
This restaurant in a stone coach house, circa 1860, offers
traditional Egyptian dishes. Belly dancers entertain Friday
and Saturday nights. Open lunch Tuesday to Friday from
noon to 3 p.m. Dinner daily from 5 p.m. to midnight.
Average prices.

French

Chanterelles, L'Hotel, 225 Front St. West.
Tel: 597-1400. Elegant decor. Nouvelle Cuisine. Extensive
wine list. Above average prices. Open lunch and dinner
Monday to Saturday.
La Chaumiere, 77 Charles St. East. Tel: 922-0500.

Toronto's first French restaurant still offering excellent traditional and Nouvelle Cuisine dishes. Lunch and dinner Monday to Saturday. Medium prices.

La Grenouille, 2387 Yonge St. Tel: 481-3093.
Traditional French cuisine. Open daily, lunch and dinner. Medium prices.

Sanssouci, Sutton Place Hotel, 955 Bay St.
Tel: 924-6068.
Haute-cuisine. Classical piano entertainment nightly. Excellent wine list. Open Monday to Saturday, lunch and dinner. Sunday brunch. Medium to expensive.

Winter Palace, The Sheraton Centre, 123 Queen St. West.
Tel: 361-1000. On the 43rd. floor, this restaurant features a menu of dishes traditional prepared by French chefs for Russian Czars. Open daily, lunch and dinner. Extensive wine list. Medium to expensive prices.

German

Gasthaus Schrader, 120 Church St. Tel: 364-0706.
Specialties include venison and wild boar. German country inn atmosphere. Open daily with entertainment and dancing on Sunday. Medium prices.

Greek

Aphrodite, 1206, Danforth Avenue. Tel: 461-5939.
Bistro-style with contemporary hi-tech decor. From an open kitchen comes barbecued and other Greek favourites plus some western dishes. Open Monday to Wednesday 9 a.m. to 2 a.m. for breakfast, lunch and dinner. Thursday to Saturday to 4 a.m. Sunday 11 a.m. to midnight. Medium prices.

Mykonos, 625, Yonge St. Tel: 925-8903. Authentic atmosphere and traditional food. Live bouzouki music plus dancing Friday and Saturday nights. Open Monday to Thursday noon to 11 p.m. Friday to midnight. Saturday 5 p.m. to midnight. Sunday 5 p.m. to 11 p.m. Medium prices.

Hungarian

Hungarian Hut Restaurant and Tavern, 127, Yonge St. Tel: 864-9275. Traditional Hungarian dishes. Romantic dinner music. Open daily for lunch and dinner. Moderate prices.

Indian

The Moghal, 563 Bloor St. est. Tel: 535-3315.
Also at 33 Elm St. Tel: 597-0522. Traditional vegetarian and non-vegetarian dishes and Tandoori cooking in an authentic Indian atmosphere. Open daily for dinner only. Medium prices.

Indonesian

Java Restaurant, 105, Church St. Tel: 364-7666.
Traditional Indonesian menu including 20-30 dish rijsttafel. Open daily, lunch and dinner. Medium prices.

Indonesia Restaurant, 678, Yonge St. Tel: 967-0697. Authentic Indonesian menu, including rijsttafel, plus vegetarian offerings. Cosy atmosphere. Open for lunch and dinner daily. Moderate prices.

International

Top Of Toronto, CN Tower, 301, Front St. West.
Tel: 362-5411. Large international menu in the world's highest revolving restaurant. Excellent wine list. Complimentary access to Sparkles Nightclub. Open daily lunch and dinner, plus Sunday brunch. Average to expensive.

Irish

McVeigh's, New Windsor Tavern, 124, Church St.
Tel: 364-9698. Irish-owned and operated, this pub has lunch and also finger foods at night with imported Irish beers and spirits. Live Irish entertainment nightly. Open daily 11.30 a.m. to 1 a.m. Medium prices.

Italian

Gran Festa Ristorante, 146 Front St. West.
Tel: 979-2020. A Toronto-famous, nine-course Italian dinner with live music in an Italian country village atmosphere. Lunch Monday to Friday. Dinner nightly from 5 p.m. to 11 p.m. Inexpensive.

Remo's Ristorante, 156 Front St. West. Tel: 596-7360. Homemade pasta, provimi veal, fresh fish and seafood, Italian-style. Open Wednesday to Saturday only for lunch and dinner. Live entertainment with dinner. Cheap to moderate.

Japanese

Asahi Gardens, 614 Jarvis St. Tel: 920-4333. Teriyaki cuisine. Sushi bar. Geisha-style service to 39 individual, small dining rooms. Lunch Monday to Saturday. Dinner nightly. Average prices.

Tanaka Of Tokyo, 1180 Bay St. Tel: 964-3868. Authentic Japanese decor and dishes. Sushi bar. Open lunch and dinner daily. Medium to average prices.

Kosher

Milk 'n Honey, 3457 Bathurst St. Tel: 789-7651. Modern decor and fish and dairy-food dinners. Open daily, lunch and dinner. Medium prices.

Mexican

Tijuana Donna's Willow Restaurant, 193 Danforth Avenue. Tel: 469-5315. Great Mexican meals served in three dining rooms and an open patio during summer. More than 70 items on the menu. Open daily for lunch and dinner. Special weekend brunch. Medium to average prices.

Moroccan

The Sultan's Tent, 1280 Bay St. Tel: 961-0601. Traditional Moroccan menu. Belly dancer entertainment. Open Monday to Saturday from 5.30 p.m. Medium to average prices.

Peruvian

The Boulevard Cafe, 161 Harbord St. Tel: 961-7676. Peruvian decor and up-market South American dishes. Open daily 11 a.m. to 1 a.m. Medium to expensive prices.

Polish

Izba Restaurant, 648 The Queensway. Tel: 251-7177. Traditional Polish dishes. Live piano and violin entertainment. Open daily for lunch and dinner. Inexpensive.

Portuguese

Ramboia Cafe and Grill, 1282 Dundas St. West. Tel: 534-0407. Fresh fish, seafood and rice dishes prepared Portuguese style. Open for lunch and dinner daily. Average prices.

Scandinavian

Vikings Dining Room, 5, St. Nicholas St. Tel: 922-1071.
A large menu of fine Scandanavian dishes. Open daily,
lunch and dinner. Moderate prices.

Seafood

The Mermaid Seafood House, 330 Dundas St. West. Tel:
597-0077. A true seafood establishment operating for
more than a quarter of a century, this restaurant continues
to present classic European seafood dishes. Open for
lunch and dinner daily. Moderate to expensive.
Lobster Trap, 1962 Avenue Rd. Tel: 787-3211. Offering
lobster in seven different sizes throughout the year. Open
daily for dinner from 5 p.m. Medium to expensive.
Spinnaker's Restaurant, 207 Queen's Quay West.
Tel: 362-3406.
Fresh fish and seafood menu changes daily. Superb view
of the waterfront. Open daily for lunch and dinner.
Moderate to average prices.

Spanish

Don Quijote Restaurante, 300 College St.
Tel: 922-7636. Traditional atmosphere and classic Spanish
dishes with optional prixe fixe menu. Open for lunch
Monday to Friday and dinner daily. Closed Sunday.
Medium prices.

Steak Restaurants

Hayloft Sirloin Pit and Tavern, 37 Front St. East.
Tel: 364-1974. Central and popular, also with seafood and
bake shop. Open daily for lunch and dinner. Medium to
expensive.
Barberian's Steakhouse, 7 Elm St. Tel: 597-0225. Set in a
pre-Confederation building with works by pioneering The
Group Of Seven and other Canadian artists. Seafood and
after-theatre dishes with fondue and souffle are also
available. Open for lunch Monday to Friday and daily dinner
from 5 p.m. to 1 a.m. Medium to expensive prices.

Swiss

The Terrace Restaurant, 123 Front St. Tel: 366-8199.
Many specials such as veal, salmon, lamb, prawns, rosti-
potatoes, etc. Open for breakfast, lunch and dinner
Monday to Friday. Lunch and dinner Saturday and Sunday.
Average to expensive.

Fort York, Toronto

Thai

Bangkok Garden, 18 Elm St. Tel: 977-6748. Award-winning Thai cuisine presented in an exotic decor. Specialties include seafood and curries. Open daily for lunch and dinner. Expensive.

Ukranian

Ukranian Caravan Restaurant-Cabaret, 5245 Dundas St. West. Tel: 231-7447. Superb traditional Ukranian dishes plus Continental offerings. Nightly cabaret features Cossack dancers. Open daily. Inexpensive without the show, but average to expensive with it.

Vegetarian

The Vegetarian Restaurant, 542 Yonge St.
Tel: 961-9522. Vegetarian dishes in both North American and International styles. Also at 2849 Dundas St. West. Tel: 762-1204. Non- smoking restaurants. Open daily lunch and dinner. Inexpensive to moderate prices.

Vietnamese

Saigon Star, 4 Collier St. Tel: 922-5840. French-style Viet-
namese dishes in an intimate atmosphere. Open daily for
lunch and dinner. Cheap to moderate prices.

Toronto Nightlife

In addition to the comedy and theatre restaurants
mentioned previously, (under Entertainment) Toronto has
a wide selection of clubs, pubs, lounges and nightclubs,
not to mention its plays, musicals, orchestral concerts,
ballet, opera, jazz, rock 'n roll and other musical presentations. There is always something going on at night along
the harbour and on it in summer. The latter can include
night dinner-dance cruises.

Major hotels and many restaurants also feature night
entertainment and this could be as diverse as a Solve The
Crime evening to dinner time entertainment or piano bar
relaxation. Hotels with theme evenings change them
frequently. Here is an example of some of the night
diversions you can enjoy in Toronto.

Lounges

Black Knight Lounge, Royal York Hotel, 100 Front St. West. Tel: 368-2511. Dining and dancing in medieaval surrounds. Open dinner Monday to Saturday. Cover charge non-guests.

Brandy Tree, Prince Hotel, 900 York Mills Rd. Tel: 444-2511. Picture windows look out to a ravine. Dancing Monday to Saturday. Open 5.30 p.m. to 1 a.m.

The Roof Garden Bar, Holiday Inn Downtown, 89 Chestnut St. Tel: 977-0707. Intimate, revolving rooftop bar with city views, live entertainment and dancing. Tuesday to Saturday from 6 p.m.

Nightclubs

Brandy's, 58, The Esplanade. Tel: 364-6674. Good for singles. Open from 9 p.m. nightly.

Berlin, 2335 Yonge St. Tel: 489-7777. Spacious, two-level club with dancing nightly. Shows Wednesday to Saturday 10 p.m. and midnight; Sunday 7 p.m. and 11 p.m. Reservation for dinner.

Misty's, Toronto Airport Hilton, 5875, Airport Rd. Tel: 677-9900. Tops for the latest in sound, light and video systems. Open nightly.

Dr. Livingstone's, Bristol Place Hotel, 950, Dixon Rd. Tel: 675-9444. African decor and atmosphere. Live entertainment and dancing from 9 p.m. nightly.

Le Strip, 237A, Yonge St. Tel: 863-0001. Continuous burlesque afternoons and nightly.

Piano Bars

Ground Floor Lounge, Plaza II Hotel, 90, Bloor St. East. Tel: 961-8000. Meet the locals here.

La Serre, Four Seasons Hotel, 21, Avenue Rd. Tel: 964-0411. Yorkeville Ave. aspect. Elegant Victorian piano bar with other entertainers.

Verandah Lounge, Guild Inn, 201 Guildwood Parkway. Tel: 261-3331. Old Toronto architectural theme. Pianist from 9 p.m.

Dinner Theatres

His Majesty's Feast, 1926, Lakeshore Boulevard West. Windemere.
Tel: 769-1165. Three hours of dining and hilarity in the simulated court of King Henry VIII. Open Tuesday to Saturday from 8 p.m.with Friday's show starting at 8.30 p.m. Reservations. Prices from medium upwards.

New York Hotel Dinner Theatre, 1150, Queen St. West.
Tel: 533-0046. Musical theatre and cabaret. Show only or dinner-show packages. Italian, steak and seafood dishes. Reservations. Open Monday to Thursday for dinner from 6.30 p.m. Show, 8.30 p.m. Friday and Saturday, dinner from 6 p.m. and 8 p.m. Shows at 8 p.m. and 10.30 p.m. Expensive.

Limelight Dinner Theatre, 2026 Yonge St. Tel: 482-5200. Dinner packages with musical show. Open Monday to Friday for dinner from 6 p.m. Show at 8 p.m. Saturday, dinner from 5 p.m. Shows at 7 p.m. and 10.30 p.m.

Jazz Clubs

East 85th, 85 Front St. East. Tel: 860-0011. New York-style jazz club with Carribean restaurant. Open for dinner daily.
My Place, 14 Market St. Tel: 860-1378. Dinner with evening jazz band. Reservations.

There are hundreds of more venues embracing every above category waiting for you to discover in swinging Toronto.

Pubs

Wheat Sheaf Pub, 667, King St. West. Tel: 364-3996. Toronto's oldest pub, 1849. Popular with sportspeople. Hearty food and inexpensive.

Elephant & Castle Pub and Restaurant, Eaton Centre, 218 Yonge St. Tel: 598-4455. From darts to dancing, this pub is a re-creation of an English country pub. Antiques, informal dining and affordable.

Scotland Yard, 56, The Esplanade. Tel: 364-6572.
DJ plays UK rock and new wave. Dancing Monday to Saturday from 9 p.m.

Windsurfing, Georgian Bay

Niagara Falls

Restaurants and Night Life

In addition to the tower restaurants mentioned in the tour section of this InfoGuide, here are a few more recommendations.

Table Rock Restaurant, The brink of the Canadian falls above the Table Rock scenic tunnels. Tel: 354-3631.

Victoria Park Restaurant, Queen Victoria Park.
Tel: 356-2217. Opposite American Falls with three meals daily on a patio overlooking it.

The Brock, the Old Stone Inn, 5425 Robinson St.
Tel: 357-1234. Intimate, French cuisine in sophisticated surroundings.

Happy Wanderer Restaurant, 6405 Stanley Avenue. Tel: 354-9825.
Largest German restaurant on the Niagara Peninsula with traditional Bavarian food.

Hungarian Village, 5329 Ferry St. Tel: 356-2429. Hungarian, Continental and steak restaurant with nightly gypsy entertainment.

Suisha Gardens, 3rd level, Village Mall, Maple Leaf Village. Tel: 357-2660. Japanese grills prepared at table.

Jade Gardens, 5306 Victoria Avenue. Tel: 356-0336. Cantonese and Szechuan menu with Chinese smorgasbord July to September.

Theatre On The Square, 3710 Main St. Tel: 295-4358. Dining followed by plays, musicals and reviews.

Rumours Nighclub and Cafe, top of Clifton Hill.
Tel: 358-6152. Casual dining and top 40 and dance nightly at the club.

Photography

Canada is a shutter-bug's paradise in every season. For information on Ontario's amazing autumn colours and its spring blossoms, call Ontario Travel on 963-2992 for 24 hour recorded reports.

Shopping

The problem with shopping in Canada, Ontario, and Toronto in particular, is not what to buy but what not to buy. Toronto, with its thousands of shops, from expensive Yorktown boutiques to its maze of underground stores and colourful, inexpensive markets, provides a shopper's paradise more than equal to any other in the world.

Canadian handicrafts and native products of artistic and/ or souvenir value to the visitor, may be high on your list of priorities. These include Inuit (Eskimo) art, moccasins, garments and novelties along with wood carvings, jewellery, hand-woven and knitted goods and glass and pottery. Leather goods sold in Toronto are of excellent quality and style. Furs are available.

> **INFOTIP:** Check with your own customs whether products from endangered species are able to be imported home.

Not only does Canada sell just about every manufactured type of article produced in the world, it also imports high-quality goods, notably from France and other European and Asian countries. So, if you cannot get to Paris, be on the lookout for articles with a Made In France label. But expect to pay more for some imported articles.

Algonquin Prov. Park

Foreigners, who do not have sales tax separately calculated and added to the purchase price at home, may find it initially unnerving that the price shown on the receipt is more than that on the price tag.

Toronto's major department stores are as follows:
Eaton's, 290 Yonge St. This is an enormous Eaton flagship store, one of 11 in Metro Toronto alone and leading to the 1000-store complex beneath the street.

Simpsons. The major branch of this department store chain is at the corner of Queen and Yonge Streets and open 24 hours. There are 10 other stores. Tel: 861-9111.

Honest Ed's, 581 Bloor St. West. Tel: 537-1574. This is the Mirvish bargain merchandise store which includes Mirvish Village for local artisans and six Mirvish restaurants.

Markets

While most of the markets feature food, which will interest you if you are shopping for your own picnic, naturally they contain shops and stalls which offer things such as art, antiques, novelties, souvenirs, jewellery, books, clothing etc. These extra goods may very in style or tradition of the ethnic area in which the market is situated.

Kensington Market occupies an old neighbourhood shared by orientals, Italians, Portuguese, West Indian and Eastern European Jews, plus many other nationalities.

Chinatown is centred around Dundas and Spadina Streets and is expanding. You will find Italian groceries and other items on College Street and other streets running to Bathurst Street. For Greek emporia, stroll along Danforth Street. The St. Lawrence Farmers' Market is at Front and Jarvis Streets.

The most chic of shops are around Bloor Street and the fascinating lanes and ways of Yorkville. Fashion Street is Spadina Avenue.

> **INFOTIP:** Canadian clothing sizes differ from those of Europe and Britain. Always try on garments before purchasing. Women's clothing has a standard range 5/6 to 20. Pullovers are usually small (S) medium (M) large (L) and extra large (XL)

The only stores of which there are not a huge proliferation are liquor stores. Liquor and imported wines and beer can be bought from government liquor stores. Domestic wines are available from retail wine shops and, if you are visiting wineries on the Niagara Peninsula, the wineries themselves.

The harbour complexes have scores of specialty shops while most musea have super gift shops offering quality souvenirs and crafts appropriate to the period of representation.

Opening Hours

In most areas of Toronto, shops are open from 9 a.m. to 5.30 or 6 p.m. although, depending on local bylaws, some remain open weekday evenings and/or weekends till late. But it is for sure that you will not go without the item you need as the city has so many shops.

> **INFOTIP:** Should you be in any sort of shopping quandry, help is only a telephone call away on 296-4416 - Shoppers' Assistance.

Duty Free

Pearson International Airport has a duty-free shop and, for those entering from the USA to Niagara Falls, there is one located at 5726 Falls Avenue.

> **INFOTIP:** American visitors returning home after 48 hours can take with them US$400 of goods every 30 days. This can include 1 litre of alcohol, 200 cigarettes or 100 cigars, provided they are not Cuban. If the stay is less than 48 hours, US$25 of goods can be bought.

Antiquities

Exporting from Canada items more than 50 years old, of historical, scientific or cultural significance is restricted. For specific information, contact The Secretary, Canadian Cultural Property Export Revue Board, Department of Communications, Ottawa, Ontario, Canada, K1A 0C8.

Sports and Athletics

Canadians are very sports orientated, be it in summer when visitors are drawn to Lake Ontario for sailing and swimming (in pools) with the locals or in crisp winter when cross-country skiing, walking in snow shoes and tobogganing is such fun in the ravines just out of downtown. One can even skate in the park of City Hall.

Almost every sport can be enjoyed in Toronto. For those not listed, check the daily newspapers and Torono Annual Visitors Guides and updates published by the Metropolitan Toronto Convention and Visitors Association. These are available at your hotel or on newstands.

ATHLETICS Ontario Colleges Athletic Association, 111, Merton St. Tel: 489-1608.

BOATING See also Tours. Ontario Travel (Tel: 965-4008) publishes an Ontario/Canada Boating guide which lists marina and boat rentals throughout Ontario.

CURLING Watch the newspapers for annoucements of dates and venues in the curling season late autumn and early spring.

> **INFOTIP:** You can watch this sport at The Terrace, 70, Mutual St. from a glass-fronted viewing room while enjoying a drink.

FISHING In trout season, fishing can be done at Metro Toronto and other conservation areas. A sports fishing licence is required. Tel: 661-6600.

Adams Charter Service, 2218, Kennedy Rd, Scarborough. Tel: 261-4997. Six-hour fishing charters on Lakes Ontario and Lake Simcoe for trout and salmon between April and October, all week. Equipment supplied.

Sport Fishing Centre, Spadina Quay, Harbourfront. Tel: 869-3474.

Fishing twice daily on Lake Ontario in season. Tackle and lures supplied.

A special fishing permit is required to fish in all Canada's national parks. These can be obtained at any national park for a small fee and are valid throughout Canada.

INFOTIP: If you are intending to visit British Columbia before or after your Ontario holiday, you must gain a tidal waters sports fishing licence to enjoy the sport in B.C. Gain information from the Department of Fisheries and Oceans, Communications Branch, 1090, West Pender St., Vancouver, British Columbia, Canada, V6E. Tel: (604) 666-1384.

FOOTBALL Canadian Football League, 1200, Bay St. Tel: 928-1200.

GOLF There are several golf clubs which will welcome visitors. These include:-
Glen Abbey Golf Club, Oakville. Tel: 844-1800. Designed by Jack Nicklaus, this is home of the Canadian Open. There are extensive facilities - and Sunday brunch.
Golf Plus, 12, Main S6t. North, Markham. Tel: 294-3076. Many facilities.
Royal Canadian Golf Association, 696, Yonge St. Tel: 925-4397.

Off to the Mountains

HUNTING Hunting licences are compulsory. In Ontario, they can be bought from the Ministry of Natural Resources, Public Information Centre, 99 Wellesley St. West. As open season dates alter seasonally and regionally, check current dates, regulations and fees in advance.

SKIING Try it at the Toronto Zoo where tuition is available. For more information on cross country skiing and alpine skiing throughout the whole province, contact Ontario Travel on Tel.963-2911.

SWIMMING Many hotels have swimming pools and along the lakeshore are several public pools.

TENNIS Downtown Tennis & Nautilus Club, 21, Eastern Ave. Tel: 362-2439. Courts, aerobics and fitness centre as well.

There are also free courts on Toronto Islands.

WALKING Toronto On Foot, 39, Leuty Ave. Tel: 690-1396. Guided walks through the city's past and present.

Also the University of Toronto has free one-hour walking tours. Tel: 978-5000.

Spectator Sports

Toronto Blue Jays Baseball Club, Skydome, 277 Front St. West. Tel: 963-3515. Member of the American League Eastern Division, the Blue Jays play many home games between April and November.

HOCKEY Toronto Maple Leafs' home is Maple Leaf Gardens, 60 Carlton St, Toronto. Tel: 977-1641.

HORSE RACING Woodbine Race Track, Highway 27 at Rexdale Boulevard, Etobicoke. Tel: 675-6110. Greenwood Race Track, 1669 Queen St. East. Tel: 698-3131.

Telephone and Telegraph

Either blue or red public telephones are on street corners, in public buildings and hotel lobbies. From them, you can make both local and long distance calls. Instructions for use are in each booth or adjacent to the telephone. You are never far away from a phone in Toronto.

To make an overseas call, you can seek the assistance of your hotel operator. Quality hotels have direct dial systems to allow you to call other countries.

For direct dialling internationally, these are the international codes from Canada for the following countries:

Argentina - 01154.
Australia - 01161.
Austria - 01143.
Belgium - 01132.
Brazil - 01155.
Cyprus - 011357.
Denmark - 01145.
Egypt - 01120.
Fiji - 011679.
West Germany - 01149.
Finland - 011358.
France - 01133.
Greece - 01130.
Hong Kong - 011852.
Iceland - 011354.
India - 01191.
Indonesia - 01162.
Ireland - 011353.
Israel - 011972.

Italy - 01139.
Japan - 01181.
Malaysia - 01160.
Malta - 011356.
Mexico - 01152.
Netherlands - 01131.
New Zealand - 01164.
Norway - 01147.
Pakistan - 01192.
Phillipines - 01163.
Portugal - 011351.
Singapore - 01165.
South Africa - 01127.
Spain 01134.
Sweden - 01146.
Switzerland - 01141.
Thailand - 01166.
United Kingdom - 01144.
USA - 0111.

After you have dialled the country code, dial the area code within that country, followed by the local number.

INFOTIP: If there are other countries not listed here that you wish to call direct, simply dial 0 and ask the operator for the route and area codes.

Time

Six of the world's 24 time zones are extended across Canada with a difference between Pacific and Atlantic Coasts of four and a half hours. Daylight Saving Time, meaning an hour later than Standard Time, begins the last Sunday in April and ends on the last Sunday in October.

Toronto is in the Eastern Standard Time Zone which is three hours behind Pacific Coast time and 90 minutes ahead of Newfoundland Standard Time - the easternmost time zone in the nation.

Tipping

If a tip or service charge is not added to your bill in Canada, generally 15 per cent of the total amount should be offered. Tipping applies to waiters, waitresses, hairdressers, barbers, taxi drivers etc. Doormen, bellhops and porters at hotels, airports and railway station are usually paid one dollar for each item carried.

Tourist Services

Province Of Ontario Travel Information Centres are open from 8 a.m. to 8 p.m. from mid-May to Labour Day which falls in the first week of September. For the rest of the year they are open between 8.30 a.m. and 4.30 p.m.

Toronto locations are

Toronto Eaton Centre, Level One, 220 Yonge St. Also at 900 Bay St, 1st Floor, Macdonald Block. Tel: 965-4008 (or, if you prefer to speak French, 965-3488.)

If you are calling from other parts of Canada (with the exception of the Yukon, North West Territories and Alaska) Tel 1-800-268-3735. For French speakers,
Tel. 1-800-268-3736. These numbers are toll-free.

For more free travel information, you can contact Ontario Ministry of Tourism and Recreation, 77, Bloor St. West. Tel: 965-9991.

Also, the **Metropolitan Toronto Convention** and **Visitors Association**, 207 Queen's Quay. Tel: 368-9990. Call also 368-9821 weekdays between 8.30 a.m. and 5 p.m. and 10 a.m. to 5 p.m. weekends. There is a MTCVA booth in front of the Eaton Centre, corner of Dundas and Yonge Streets and booths at the CN Tower, Metro Toronto Zoo and Ferry Docks (Queen's Quay,) which are open between June 18 and September 5, Monday to Saturday 9 a.m. to 7 p.m.and 9.30 a.m. to 6 p.m. Sundays. Booths at Toronto City Hall and Royal Ontario Museum are open daily May 14 to September 5. Times are Monday to Saturday 9 a.m. to 7 p.m. and Sundays 9.30 a.m. to 6 p.m. Sundays.

In **Niagara Falls**, contact Niagara Falls, Canada, Visitor and Convention Bureau, 4673 Ontario Avenue, Niagara Falls. Tel: 356-6061.

Information on tourism in other Canadian provinces other than Ontario, can be obtained from the following:

Alberta - Travel Alberta, Box 2500, Edmonton, Alberta. Tel: 1-800-661-8888. (Toll free)

British Columbia - Tourism British Columbia, 1117 Wharf St, Victoria, British Columbia. Tel: (604) 387-6147.

Manitoba - Travel Manitoba, Department 5020, Legislative Building, Winnipeg, Manitoba. Tel: 1-800-665-0040. (Toll free)

New Brunswick - Tourism New Brunswick, P.O. Box 12345, Federation, New Brunswick. Tel: 1-800-561-0123. (Toll free)

Newfoundland - Tourism Branch, department of Development, Box 2016, St. John's, Newfoundland. Tel: (709) 737-2830.

North West Territories - TravelArctic, Yellowknife, North West Territories. Tel: (403) 873-7200.

Nova Scotia - Department of Tourism, P.O. Box 130, Halifax, Nova Scotia. Tel: 1-800-565-7140. (Toll free.)

Prince Edward Island - Visitor Services Division, Department of Finance and Tourism, P.O. Box 940, Charlottetown, Prince Edward Island. Tel: 1-800-561-0123.
Toll free.

Quebec - Tourisme Quebec, C.P. 20 000, Quebec, Quebec. Tel: 1-800-361-6490. (Toll free)

Saskatchewan - Tourism Saskatchewan, 2103, 11th Avenue, Regina, Saskatchewan. Tel: 1-800-667-5822. (Toll free)

Yukon - Tourism Yukon, P.O. Box 2703, Whitehorse, Yukon. Tel: (403) 667-5430.

INFOTIP: Provincial, municipal and regional tourist information offices are numerous throughout Ontario and other parts of Canada. You can see signs indicating their locations on roads and they are often indicated on provincial highway maps.

National Parks and Reserves _____

Information on the parks, reserves, hunting and fishing regulations, licences, angling conditions and game species in every province and territory of Canada can be gained from National Parks of Canada, Parks Canada, Ottawa, Ontario, Canada K1A 1G2.

Outside Canada, the Canadian Government maintains offices in many countries and can provide the prospective visitor with up to date information. Canadian High Commissions, Embassies and Consulates worldwide will offer valuable information on travelling to and within Canada.

Australia, Canadian Consulate General, 8th floor, AMP Centre, 50 Bridge St, Sydney, N.S.W. 2000.

Japan. Canadian Embassy (Annex) Yamakatsu Building, 5-32, Akasaka 8-chome, Minato-ku, Tokyo 107.

Hong Kong, Commission For Canada, 14/15th floors, Asian House, 1, Hennessy Rd, or P.O. Box 20264, Hennessy Road Post Office.

Italy, Canadian Consulate General, Via Vittor Pisani 19, 20124 Milan.

France, Ambassade du Canada, 37, Avenue Montaigne, 75008, Paris.

West Germany, Canadisches Fremdenverkehrsamt, Biebergasse 6-10, D-6000, Frankfurt-on-Main.

The Netherlands, Canadese Ambassade, Afdeling Handelsbetrekkingen, Sophialaan 7, 2514 JP, Den Haag.

Mexico, Canadian Embassy, Calle Schiller 529, Colonia Polanco, Mexico 5, DF.

United Kingdom, Canadian High Commission, Canada House, Trafalgar Square, London SW1Y 5BJ.

Tours

Toronto has many tour operators offering a variety of sightseeing experiences. Here is a selection of them. You will find many more of them in the Yellow Pages of the Toronto telephone directory, in newspaper advertisements and tourist publications.

Water Tours Adventures Afloat, Pier 6, bottom of York St. Tel: 368-2358. Sixty and 90 minute cruises. Also charter yacht cruises.

Baccarat Yacht Charters, 123, Edward St. Tel: 595-5737. Luxury 35 metre yacht cruises. Murder mystery cruises. Dancing. Bars.

The Challenge, 207 Queen's Quay West. Tel: 366-2626. Tall ship cruising under sail. Bar. Dinner dance cruises. Free shuttle from Union Station.

Classic Yacht Charters and Sails, 145 Queen's Quay West. Tel: 360-6078 (winter) and 861-0437. Luxury motor yacht. Sightseeing, picnics and barbecues.

The Oriole, moored south side of 207 Queen's Quay West. Tel: 366-2626. Inner harbour tour on Victorian-style river boat. Bar. One hour tours April to October. Also summer dinner dance cruises Sundays. Free shuttle from Union Station.

The Trillium, Island Ferry docks down from Bay St. Tel: 392-8194. 1910, steam-powered, side-paddle ferry boat, unique in North America. One hour or 90 minutes cruises.

Gray Line Harbour and Island Tours, 5 Queen's Quay West. Tel: 364-2412. Amsterdam-style glass-top tour boats. One hour trips.

There are several other water cruise operators.
Bus: Gray Line Sightseeing Bus Tours, Bus Terminal,
610 Bay St Tel: 979-3511. Tours from terminal and major
downtown and midtown hotels. Also tours outside
Toronto.

Happy Day Tours, 220 Yonge St. South, Aurora. Tel: 593-6220.
Four-hour city tours and Black Creek from all airport hotels
and many downtown.

Toronto Sites, 31, Parkview Gardens. Tel: 247-1544.
Personalized tours.

Toronto By Trolleycar, 134 Jarvis St. Tel: 869-1372. Old
fashioned trolleycar tour of the city.

Rickshaw: Velvet Wheels Rickshaws, 600 Spadina
Avenue.
Tel: 532-2803.
Walking tours: University of Toronto Historic Walking
Tours, University of Toronto, Map Room, Hart House, just
off Queens Park Crescent West. Free one hour tours of
Canada's largest and historical university.

Toronto On Foot, 39 Leuty Avenue. Tel: 690-1396. Conducted walks.

Air: Toronto Downtown Heliport, 55 Unwin Avenue. Tel: 461-4633. Helicopter rides. Sightseeing flights. Charters to Niagara Falls and other attractions.

Niagara Falls Tours

From Toronto: Niagara Tours, 134 Jarvis St. Tel: 868-0400. Daily coach or minibus tours including lunch, year round.

(See also above Gray Line Tours and Happy Day Tours.)

In Niagara Falls: Ontario's Niagara Parks Package Tour. Tel: 356-7633. Daily tours operate from tour booths near the falls from mid-May to mid-October. Tour includes double-decker bus trip, Table Rock Scenic Tunnels, Maid Of The Mist boat tour, Great Gorge trip and Spanish Aero Car ride, plus lunch and other attractions.

Niagara Helicopters, Niagara Parkway. Tel: 357-5672.

Lake Ontario

THE METRIC SYSTEM

Length

1 millimetre	0.04 inches
1 centimetre	0.39 inches
1 metre	1.09 yards
1 kilometre	0.62 mile

Converting kilometres to miles is as simple as multiplying the number of kilometres by 0.62.(e.g. 10km's x 0.62 6.2 miles)

Converting miles to kilometres is done by multyplying the number of miles by 1.61 (e.g. 60mi x 1.61 96.6km's)

Capacity

1 litre	33.92 ounces
	1.06 quart
0.26 gallons	

Converting litres to gallons, multiply the num'er of litres by .26. (e.g. 20l x .26 5.2 gallons)

Converting gallons to litres multiply number of gallons by 3.79. (e.g. 10 gal x 3.79 37.9l)

Weight

1 gram 0.04 ounces
1 kilogram 2.2 pounds

Converting kilograms to pounds, multiply number of kilos by 2.2. (e.g. 55 kg x 2.2 121 pounds)

Converting pounds to kilograms, multiply number of pounds by .45. (e.g. 100 pounds x .45 45 kilos)

Area

1 hectare 10000m/sqr or 2.47 acres

Converting hectares to acres, multiply the number of hectares by 2.47 (e.g. 10 ha x 2.47 24.7 acres)

Converting acres to hectares, multiply the number of acres by .41 (e.g. 40 acres x .41 16.4 ha)

Temperature

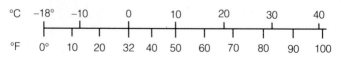

°C	−18°	−10		0		10		20		30		40	
°F	0°	10	20	32	40	50	60	70	80	90	100			

Ottawa

Nathan Philips Square

PART V
Business Guide

Niagara-On-The Lake

BUSINESS GUIDE

Contents

Banks
Business Briefing
Business Publications
Business Services
Business-Trade Organizations
Conference Facilities
Credit Cards
Currency Exchange
Export
Expositions,Trade Fairs and Exhibitions
Import/Export of Currency
Messenger Services
Social Business Associations
Translators and Interpreters

Business Briefing

Main Industries: Heavy machinery, aviation, automobiles, electrical goods, electronic goods, urban transport systems, iron and steel, mining, chemicals and petroleum, agricultural products, fishing and forestry.
Main exports: Manufactured products (two thirds being automobiles and automotive parts,) petroleum, chemicals, pulp and paper, iron and steel, dairy products, heavy machinery and office equipment, aircraft, diesel trains and wheat.
Main imports: Vehicle parts excluding mortors, electronic software, apparel and accessories, telecommunications and related equipment.
Principal trading partners: USA, Japan.

Exchange, Import/Export of Currency

There is no limit on the import of currency into Canada. Exporting large amounts, one must inform the Bank of Canada.

Banks

Foreign and Canadian banks open from 10 a.m. to 3 p.m. Monday to Friday. Some banks have extended hours. Large hotels will exchange travellers' cheques in foreign currencies but the rate will be lower and, as mentioned previously, if you do not have travellers' cheques in Canadian dollars you will pay a significant surcharge.

Visitors who are conducting business in Canada may need Letters Of Credit from their banks in their home country. Major banks will have corresponding relationships with Canadian banks. Canadian bankers are happy to organize necessary letters of introduction.

Foreign Banks in Toronto

Banca Commerciale Italiana of Canada, Adelaide St. West. Tel: 366-8101.
Banca Nazionale del Lavoro of Canada, 95, Wellington St. West. Tel: 365-7777.
Bank of Boston, Canada, 70, University St. Tel: 596-1784.
Bank of China Representative Office, 181, University St. Tel: 362-2991.
Banco Nacionale De Mexico,1, First Canadian Place. Tel: 368-1399.
Bank of Tokyo, Canada, Royal Bank Plaza. Tel: 865-0220.
Banque Nationale de Paris (Canada,) 36, Toronto St. Tel: 360-8040.
Barclays Bank of Canada, Commerce Court West. Tel: 862-0594.

Canadian Banks

BT Bank of Canada, Royal Bank Plaza. Tel: 865-0770.
Bank of Nova Scotia, 44, King St. West. Tel: 866-6161.
Banque Federale de Developpement, 7501, Keele St.
Tel: 738-1788.
Canadian Imperial Bank of Commerce, Commerce Court.
Tel: 980-2211.
Bank of Canada, 250, University St. Tel: 593-2000.
Bank of Montreal, First Canadian Place. Tel: 867-5000.
Canada Royal Bank, 325, Front St. West. Tel: 974-4447.

The major Canadian banks have scores of branches in
Metro Toronto. The head offices and branches are listed in
the Toronto telephone directory's yellow pages.

Credit Cards

American Express, 101, McNabb St, Unionville.
Tel: 474-8000.
Diners Club, Canada Royal Bank, 325, Front St. West.
Tel: 974-4447.
Mastercard, Bank of Montreal, First Canadian Place.
Tel: 232-8020.
Visa, Canadian Imperial Bank of Commerce, 750,
Lawrence Avenue West. Tel: 785-8090

Business-Trade Organizations

Board of Trade of Metro Toronto, 1, First Canadian Place.
Tel: 362-6811.
Canadian Manufacturers' Association, 1, Yonge St.
Tel: 363-7261.
Ontario Chamber of Commerce, 2323, Yonge St.
Tel: 482-5222.
Toronto Junior Board of Trade, First Canadian Place.
Tel: 368-1681.
World Trade Centre Toronto, 60 Harbour St. Tel: 863-2001.

Foreign Business-Trade Organizations

Brazil-Canada Chamber of Commerce, 100, Adelaide St.
West. Tel: 364-4634.
Canadian German Chamber of Industry and Commerce,
480, University St. Tel: 598-3355.

Corso Italia Business Association, 1267-A, St. Clare St. West. Tel: 652-0251.
French Chamber of Commerce for Canada, 210, Dundas St. West. Tel: 977-7119.
German-Canadian Business and Professional Association, 100, Adelaide St. West. Tel: 863-9453.
Hong Kong Trade Development Council, 347, Bay St. Tel: 336-3594.

> **INFOTIP:** As in any other large city, there are scores of specialized business associations in Toronto, covering anything from automobile parts to furs and timber products. The Ontario Chamber of Commerce and the Board of Trade (addresses and telephone numbers above,) will be able to put you in touch with any specialized trade association in the city or province. Many are also listed under Associations in the telephone directory's yellow pages.

Social Business Associations

International service clubs such as Rotary, Lions, Jaycees, etc., are represented in Toronto. These clubs invariably meet in hotels and it is best to inquire from Ontario Travel or Metropolitan Toronto Convention and Visitors Association for current venues as these can alter from time to time.

Other Organisations

The Canadian Executive Service Organization, 415, Yonge St. Tel: 596-2376.
North Toronto Business and Professional Women's Club, 3300, Yonge St. Tel: 487-9244.

Business Publications

The following is a selection of daily Toronto newspapers, and magazines and other periodicals with offices in the city which may be of assistance to the business traveller. Not all are Toronto published (e.g. Wall Street Journal.) Toronto has an enormous number of newspaper and magazine offices, some producing specialist publications on subjects from footwear to trading automobiles.

Visitors with specialized business interests are advized to check the telephone directory yellow pages under newspapers, publishers - newspapers, publishers - periodicals and magazines to find the literature most suitable for their purpose. Foreign newspapers and magazines in English and French are available and also foreign language newspapers printed in Toronto and other parts of Canada.

Newspapers:
Toronto Star. Tel: 367-2000.
Toronto Sun. Tel: 947-2222.
Toronto Globe and Mail. Tel: 585 5000.
Financial Post. Tel: 596-5148.
Financial Times of London. Tel: 283-2777.
The Economist and Sun. Tel: 495-9440.
Canada Times. Tel: 593-2777.
Wall Street Journal. Tel: 364-0674.
Women & Business. Tel: 482-2878.

Magazines and Guides:
The Blue Book of Canadian Business. Tel: 422-4742;
Small Business Magazine. Tel: 364-4760;
Time Canada, Tel: 884-2121;
Japan Economic Journal. Tel: 598-0530.
Toronto Life Magazine. Tel: 364-3333.
Business Journal Magazine. Tel: 366-7139.
Financial Times of Canada. Tel: 922-1133.
Successful Meetings,(New York published but often featuring Canada,) Telephone in Toronto is 363-1388.

Business Services

Hotels with business centres with secretarial, telex, photocopying, FAX, telephone and meeting room facilities are included in the accommodation section of this InfoGuide. Under facilities, see the initial U for meeting and convention rooms. This also indicates there are adequate business facilities.

Metropolitan Toronto Convention and Visitors' Association, being business as well as tourism orientated, will also be able to assist with advice on facilities and where to get them.

Messenger Services

Again, Toronto has dozens of messenger, courier and parcel delivery service operators. These include:-
Brothers Courier Service. (local) 251-1159.
Greyhound Courier Express, (local, inter-province and USA) Tel: 979-3511.

Canpar, (local, Canada and USA) Tel: 276-1030.
Canadian Airlines International AirCargo, (Canada and overseas) Tel: 676-3421.
Loomis Courier Service, (local, Canada, USA and overseas) Tel: 674-2000.

Expositions, Trade Shows & Fairs

A Time for Children, 2, St. Clair St. West. Tel: 963-8586.
Canada Showcase, 1001, Denison St. Tel:477-7460.
Canadian Craftshow, 21, Grenville St. Tel: 960-3680.
The Canadian High Technology Show, 36. Toronto St.
Tel: 362-5668.
Canadian National Exhibition, Exhibition Place.
Tel: 393-6000.
Canadian National Sportsmen's Shows, 595, Bay St.
Tel: 593-7333.
Canadian International Metro Festival, 263, Adelaide St. West. Tel: 977-0466.
Contemporary Craft Shows, 1008, Pape St. Tel: 429-7780.

Call the above for opening times and dates.

Also:-
Toronto Cooks, 177, St George St.
Travel and Leisure Show, 557, Christie St.
Woman's Show, 195, Bridgeland St.
Speed Sport Show, 400, Esna Park Drive.

Exports

If you have been hunting in Canada's North West Territories, you must gain a permit to export skins and trophies. Do remember that most of Canada's provincial parks and reserves prohibit weapons.

If you buy goods for export, you can claim exemption from Ontario's seven per cent Retail Sales Tax on accumulated purchases exceeding $C100 (exclusive of tax.) If your purchase is exported direct by the retailer, tax will not be added. If you carry your purchases with you, you will pay the tax, but can claim the rebate if the articles are taken from the province within 30 days. Keep original receipts indicating tax paid and date of purchase. For application forms, request the brochure Provincial Sales Tax Refunds For Visitors To Ontario, which you can obtain from many Toronto merchants and Ontario Travel. (See addresses under Tourist Services.)

Translators and Interpreters

Translators and interpreters can be found through Ontario Travel and Metropolitan Toronto Convention and Visitors' Association should you need to communicate in French or other languages.

Conference Facilities

From an International Economic Summit Conference of foreign heads of State or an international exposition with conference to a small business meeting, Toronto is well equipped to handle every type of conference possible. The province of Ontario actually hosts more meetings than anywhere else in Canada.

The facilities are too numerous to list but the venues are as varied as the huge Skydome with its unique hotel, the Canadian Exposition and Conference Centre, the Hotel Harbour Castle Westin which has its own convention centre with ballroom accommodation for 3,500 deleges and the grand, old Royal York with its 1,600 suites, 25 meeting rooms, both intimate or large enough to welcome 1,400 at a sit-down dinner.

The Georgian Bay area with its lovely lakes is about two hours drive from Toronto and has well established lodges for smaller conferences while Niagara Falls with its proliferation of closely congregated hotels and the apres-conference sports facilities of Niagara-On-The Lake is also a popular venue.

The Metropolitan Toronto Convention and Visitors' Association, 207, Queen's Quay or P.O. Box 126, Toronto, M5J 1A7. Tel: (416) 368-9990; FAX (416) 977-9930 has full information on conference planning, booking and pre and post conference pleasures.

Major airlines with offices in Toronto include:
Canadian Airlines International. Tel: 869-6721.
Canada. Tel: 925-2311.
American Airlines. Tel: 383-2203.
Northwest Airlines. Tel: 677-3412.
United Airlines. Tel: 823-2740.
US Air. Tel: 358-1913.
BWIA. Tel: 863-9595.
British Airways. Tel: 595-2616.
Japan Airlines. Tel: 364-7229.
KLM. Tel: 323-9520.
Air Toronto. Tel: 676-6222.
Ontario Express. Tel: 675-8371.

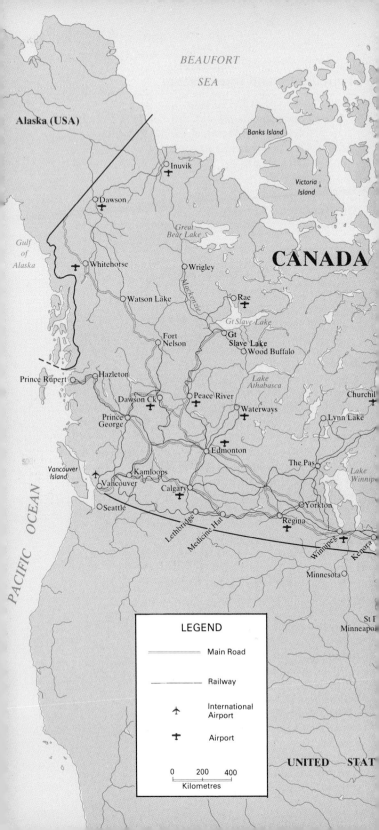

Alphabetical Index

A

Academy of Medicine 61
Advance Planning 117
African Lion Safari 80
Alexandra Bridge 93
Algonkian people 25
Allan Gardens 64
Amuseument Park 87
Animal amphitheatre 80
Antiquities 166
Art Galleries & Museums 124
Art Gallery, Ontario 54
At the Heart of it all 40
Athletics 166
Avon River 92

B

Bank of Upper Canada 68
Banks 183
Baseball Hall of Fame
          & Museum 46
Beaches Park 48
Bed and Breakfast 99
Beneath the streets 70
Bering Strait 25
Beyond Downtown 72
Black Creek Pioneer Village 74
Bookshops 144
Bridal Falls 84
Business Briefing 183
Business Guide 183
Business Services 187

C

CN Tower 37
CN Tower 50
Campbell House 54
Camping 99
Canadian Horseshoe Falls 82
Canadian Nat. Exhibition 44
Canadian National 50
Canadian National Gallery 93
Canadian People 19
Cardinal Richelieu 26
Casa Loma 61
Centreville 42
Children's Entertainment 129
China Court 56
Chinatown 56

Cinderella city 37
Cinemas 129
City Hall 54
City Hall, Toronto's First 68
City of North York 72
Clairevill Reservoir 77
Clareville Conservation Park 77
Clifton Museum 87
Climate 13
Clothing 118
Colborne Lodge 47
Commerce 17
Concovation Hall 58
Conference Facilities 189
Consulates 138
Crime 141
Currency 121
Customs 120

D

David Gibson 74
Death 140
Dinner Theatres 159
Documents 117
Dragon Mountain 82
Drake childcare Collection 61
Drugs 119
Duty Free Imports 121

E

Eaton Centre 65
Education 16
Electricity 124
Employment 118
Entertainment 124
Entry Regulations 120
Ernest Hemingway 38
Eskimos 19
Etiene Brule 30
Exchange, of Currency 183
Exhibitions 131
Exports 188

F

Far enough farm 42
Fauna 13
Festival of Lights 89
Festival of Lights 84
Festivals 132

Flora 13
Floral Clock 88
Flower City 78
Fort George 89
Fort Niagara 81
Fort Rouille 30
Fort York 46
G
Geography 12
Geology 12
George R Gardiner
          Museum 60
Getting around Outside
          Toronto 136
Getting around Toronto 135
Getting to Canada 122
Gibson House 74
Glacial Epoch 81
Goat Island 82
Government 16
Grange, The 55
Great Gorge 88
Great Lakes 13, 24
Great War Flying Museum 78
Grenadier Pond 47
Guiness Museum 87
H
Harbourfront 42
Hart House 58
Help 138
Henry Moore 54
High Park 47
Hillebrand Estate Winery 92
Historical Museum 90
Hockey Hall of Fame
          & Museum 44
Hogtown 37
Hotels 99
Hudson Bay 24
Huron tribes 26
I
IMAX Theatre 85
Igloos 24
Indoor Zoo 49
Industry 17
Insulin 38
Iroquitos nations 26
Island Miquelon 26
Island St. Pierre 26

J
Jacques Cartier 25
James Austin 62
Jazz Clubs 159
John Cabot 25
John G Howard 47
John Quay 43
John Simcoe 41
John Simcoe 30, 37
K
Kanata 25
Kayaks 24
Kiwanis Club 61
L
Lake Erie 81
Lake Huron 26
Lake Ontario 81
Lake Shore Boulevard 43
Language 21
Leif Ericsson 9
Libraries 141
Library, Metropolitan Toronto 62
Lord Simcoe 27
Lost Property 140
Lower Canada 27
M
MacKenzie House 65
Maid of the Mist 86
Maple Leaf Quay 43
Maple Leaf Village 87
Marineland 82
Maritime Museum 43
Market Gallery 69
Markets 164
Massey Hall 68
McLaughlin Planetarium 58
Medical Emergencies 140
Medical Tips 119
Meeting People 21
Mennonite quilts 75
Messenger Services 187
Metric System 176
Metropolitan Toronto 39
Minolta Tower 83
Montreal 10
Motoring 142
Museum 46
Museum of Civilization 93
Museum of the History of
          Medicine 61

Index

N

Nathan Phillips Square 54
National Aviation Museum 93
National Ballet 69
National Historic Park 89
National Park and Reserves 172
Nature boy 80
Newfies 10
Niagara Falls Museum 88
Niagara Falls 81
Niagara Gorge 86
Niagara Gorge 83
Niagara Park's Greenhouse 82
Niagara River 81
Niagara on the Lake 81
Niagara-on-the-Lake 90
Nightclubs 158
Nightlife 148-157-162

O

O'Keefe Centre 69
Odds and Ends 119
Ontario Gov. Buildings 57
Ontario Place 45
Other Organisations 186
Ottawa 10
Ottawa 92
Ottawa River 93
Out for the Day 72

P

Parliament Building 56
Photography 162
Piano Bars 158
Place Royale 26
Police Emergencies 140
Police museum, Metr. Toronto 64
Post Office 144
Post Office, Toronto's First 68
Public Holidays 134
Publications Business 186
Pubs 159

Q

Quebec 10
Queen's Bay 37

R

Radio/Television 134
Rainy River 37
Raymond Moriyamas 62
Redpath Sugar Museum 48
Religion 19
Religion Services 145

Replacement of items 140
Restaurants 148-162
Rideau Canal 10
Rideau Canal 93
Roy Thomson Hall 53
Royal Alexandra Theatre 53
Royal Ontario Museum 58
Royal York Hotel 52

S

Sam Patch 81
Samuel de Champlain 10
Scadding Cabin 45
Scarborough bluff 41
Scarborough bluffs 48
Science Centre, Ontario 72
Seminars 134
Settlement 24
Shaw Festival 91
Shopping 163
Side Tripping 79
Sigmund Samuel Building 57
Sir Henry Pellat 61
Sir John Macdonald 27
Skydome 41
Skydome 51
Skylon Tower 84
Social Bus. Associations 186
Space Deck 50
Space age 24
Spadina House 62
Spadina Quay 43
Spectator Sports 168
Spirit of Pioneering 9
Sports 166
St. Lawrence River 24
St. Lawrence Centre 68
Stanley Barracks 43
Stanley Cup 44
Statford Festival 92
Sunnyside Beach 46
Sunshine beach Water Park 77

T

Telephone and Telegraph 168
Theatre Dining 130
Theatres and Auditoria 129
Thirty Year War 26
Thule Eskimo 24
Time 169
Tipping 170
Todmorden Mills 74

Top of Toronto 50
Toronto Islands 40
Toronto Star 38
Toronto Stock Exchange 53
Toronto Zoo 49
Toronto, more than a capital 30
Tour of the Universe 50
Tourist Services 170
Tours 172-175
Trade Organizations 185
Trade shows & Fairs 188
Translators/Interpreters 189
Traveller's cheques 141
Treaty of St. Germain-en-Laye 26
Trillium 42
U
Underground City 38
University College 58
University of Toronto 58
Upper Canada 41
Upper Canada 27
Upper Canada Brewing Co. 78
V
Vaccinations 119
Vancouver 10
Vinland the Good 25
W
Waltzing Waters 84
Water's Edge Promenade 43
West Toronto 61
Wine Festival 89
Wonder of Nature's World 81
Wonderland, Canada's 76
Woodbine Race Track 77
Woodbine beach Park 48
Y
Yonge Street 30
Yorkville 62

Notes

Notes